Authentic
leadership

Authentic leadership

Discover and live your essential mission

Bas W. Blekkingh

infiniteideas

First published in 2015 by
Infinite Ideas Limited
www.infideas.com

A CIP catalogue record for this book is available from the British Library
ISBN 978–1–908984–35–7

Translated from Dutch by Business Translation Services
Designed by Bigtop Design Limited
Printed in Britain

www.authentiekleiderschap.nl/en

Contents

Foreword

This book is about you. Before we embark on our journey together let me introduce myself. I am a former army officer and regatta rower and am now leader of an organisation which unleashes and connects the hidden authentic power of leaders and their organisations. Our mission is to create high performing teams with leaders who feel extremely fulfilled. I see myself as a lucky person. I grew up in a loving warm family with parents who appreciated me and gave me the feeling that I really matter, which has given me great self-confidence. I have been given the chance to develop in a direction that lets me use my talents to the full. As a child I was fascinated by why people do the things they do. I have never lost that curiosity. The moment you know why you behave in a certain way you can speed up your development. This curiosity has taken me through some beautiful, and less beautiful, places and brought me to where I am now. I'm going to start by sharing some (perhaps strange) experiences as they form the basis of the philosophy of this book.

Experience 1 I was a regatta rower, and was selected to row at the junior world championships. There was a moment in training when we underwent a twelve minute test on a rowing machine. The number of revolutions of the machine partly decided whether you were selected for the national team or not. One rower reached the pain limit, as we all did, and cried, completely exhausted, 'I can't continue. I'm dying.' The response from the national coach was severe: 'If you think you'll die, you are still capable of thinking and can carry on for at least another half hour.' A strange remark, but I was eighteen and believed him. I really believed that this was the truth. This strange belief made me go on and on, pain or no pain. I was convinced that if the going gets tough you can unleash an inner strength which is controlled by your own belief system.

Experience 2 I joined the Royal Military Academy and became an officer in the army. It is an honourable profession and physically very challenging. I became responsible for the development of conscripts and professional leaders in the army. I joined the Royal Army Medical Corps because I realised that I would rather help people (both allies and enemies) out of trouble than put them into it. I was pretty fanatical and wanted people not only to understand but also to feel how powerful they are and how this power could be conveyed to their personnel. At the point at which these upcoming officers became physically and mentally exhausted I taught them to help others, and invariably a wondrous, previously hidden power was released that allowed them to carry on, making them extremely proud and fulfilled. It was magnificent.

Experience 3 I was a leadership trainer at a commercial organisation. We taught managers influencing skills and techniques. I found that leaders became very good at the tricks, but that in the process, they lost some of their authentic power. It was as though they had become fake in some way. I came to the conclusion that true leadership is not about learning tricks. It's about unleashing your authentic inner power and facing the fears that stop you giving yourself completely to your environment. I quit my job and started my own company.

Nowadays as an advisor and university lecturer I often work with leaders, their teams and their organisations. This has made me increasingly aware that leaders who have a lot of responsibilities are faced with a challenge. They want to develop, but have enough job-specific experience, skills and techniques. What they are searching for are ways to get more out of their job, sometimes more out of their lives. More fulfilment, more effectiveness, more of a sense that they are making a real contribution, that they are doing their job with purpose. They feel that they have a lot to share, but every now and then, something is holding them back. In the open and honest talks I have had with them I have detected two common threads: they are searching for a mission that will allow them to make an inspiring contribution to the world around them, and they are unconsciously confronted with the negative aspects of their egos. Over the years I have developed insights and methods for dealing with these issues and created a tried and tested approach which leads to greater success and happiness.

I have been struck by something else too. People often dig too deep or, conversely, not deep enough, for a solution to a problem. Moreover, leaders look for structures and guidance in order to better deal with problems. While thinking about these points I was introduced to Bateson's (1972) theory of logical levels of thinking. Although this is an interesting model, it did not fully serve my purposes. I thought it lacked something. However, it inspired me to develop my own practically applicable model: the seven-layered model. The content arose from a synthesis of study, research, practical experience, talks with colleagues and literature study. As a lecturer in Authentic Leadership at Nyenrode, I have had the opportunity to further elaborate on this model over recent years. It is my ambition to pass on insights that are effective in practice.

Authentic Leadership goes beyond management. It concerns understanding your motives and discovering your mission, with the aim of inspiring and leading yourself and others. Authentic Leadership revolves around the fundamental questions in life: Who am I really? Why am I here? What's my mission? What do I stand for? According to my dictionary, 'authentic' means 'genuine' and, therefore, 'reliable'. Your mission lies hidden within your authenticity. Your mission is what gives your life meaning, the contribution you are going to make to the world. Many people understand the concept of leadership to mean 'managing others'. However, within the context of this book, I use the term 'leadership' in the sense of 'being an influencer'. Authentic Leadership therefore amounts to 'exerting influence with your mission in mind, in a genuine and reliable way'.

You will quickly learn to work with this field-tested, seven-layered model, which you can apply to yourself as well as to others. Through case studies and a few exercises, you will undertake a reconnaissance of the seven layers of your existence. In reaching inwards, you will probably become increasingly curious about your core, your authenticity. What are your deepest motives, what mission lies behind all those layers?

Once you have found your core, you will be able to work towards the outside. Your mission will then guide your behaviour. Your problems will be cast in a different light. The model presented in this book will enable you to analyse and solve your problems. You will learn to understand your egos and you will discover and live your mission. You will learn to put Authentic Leadership into effect. Moreover, you will learn to help others to take the same steps that you are taking. These insights will therefore enable you to lead a more fulfilled and successful life.

STRUCTURE OF THE BOOK: THE SEVEN-LAYERED MODEL

The division of chapters is based on the seven-layer model with each chapter presenting the problems associated with a layer and suggesting approaches and solutions to the difficulties. Step by step, you will become acquainted with increasingly deeper layers. Chapters 1–4 provide a theoretical framework that will enable you to understand the most important insights of Chapters 5–8.

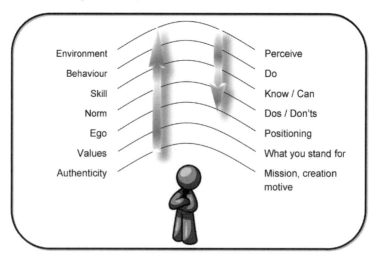

Chapter 1: The environmental layer

The outermost layer is the starting point. Most people project problems onto this layer: an obnoxious boss, a troublesome employee, a nagging neighbour, a weak government. You will come to understand that people's perception of their environment is often flawed, and is usually the result of selective perception. People who don't progress beyond this layer resort to complaining and position themselves as victims. In order to achieve Authentic Leadership, it is essential that you have an understanding of the psychological phenomenon of selective perception.

Chapter 2: The behavioural layer

This chapter explores the behaviour that you display in your environment and examines a number of psychological concepts such as self-image, self-fulfilling prophecy and self-talk. This knowledge is essential in order to be able to tackle deeper layers. You will discover what motives guide your behaviour and what results you hope to achieve which will allow you to experience the power of a strong vision. This process will raise a few questions: if I experience a problem in my environment, where does my responsibility to do something about it begin? What behavioural choices do I have? You will translate a problem from the first layer into the second, and will gain insights that will enable you to solve your problems more effectively.

Chapter 3: The skills layer

Why is it that some people can solve problems in a constructive way, while others always end up arguing? This chapter outlines ways in which you can deal with such issues and the relevant communication skills.

Chapter 4: The norms layer

What are norms, and to what extent do they influence our behaviour? Norms are often the decisive factor in whether we engage with, or ignore, a problem.

Chapter 5: The ego layer

In this chapter we will discuss what egos are, and how they function. You will discover why you unconsciously use them, what benefits and risks are involved and how you can overrule them when you realise they are not producing the results you desire. This is an important issue, since this is where you'll come up against a glass ceiling: something is obstructing your development, but you don't know what it is.

Chapter 6: The values layer

Values are the fundamental principles on which inner norms are based. The combination of norms and values in a specific environment is referred to as its 'culture'. This chapter will give you insight into the structure of a culture and how you can effectively deal with cultural conflicts. You will also explore the values that are important for your mission.

Chapter 7: The authenticity layer

This is the deepest and most important layer, the one that gives meaning to your life. This chapter deals with questions like: What is your mission? What really makes you fulfilled? What would you like to achieve? How can you operate more independently in your environment from within your 'self'? What would you like to contribute to the world around you? Why does authentic behaviour give you the best chance to achieve happiness and results?

Chapter 8: From ego to authenticity

This chapter deals with the recognition of the ego and authenticity layers and their integration. You will be shown how you can progress from ego to authenticity.

WEBSITE

In addition to the book, there is an Authentic Leadership website (www. authentiekleiderschap.nl/en). The website provides products, articles, examples of missions and an explanation of additional leadership skills.

INVITATION

I would like to invite you to go on a journey and examine yourself layer by layer. During your journey, take note of points that you can immediately put into practice. Make a note of striking events and anecdotes related to the issue of Authentic Leadership. Also try to keep track of the experiences that give you a sense of satisfaction, since this will help you to define issues in more concrete terms at a later stage.

Absorb the subject matter as a leader, not as a student. Start working on it immediately. Don't keep the subject matter to yourself. Take people along on your journey (some people select a sparring partner for their journey).

Visit the website, and follow me or our company on Twitter (@basblek-kingh and @authle respectively) to share your experiences with others. You can also find us on Facebook under 'Authentic Leadership'.

Enjoy both the journey and the destination!

Acknowledgements

Thanks to:

My wife Femke for her enthusiasm (she suggested I put my ideas down in writing), her feedforward (thanks to which I remained level-headed and did not digress too much) and her editorial support.

My children Eline and Nynke for teaching me the importance of passing on the best of yourself to others.

My parents Wim and Immy who, through their endless love, made me feel that I make a difference.

Anje-Marijcke van Boxtel who, with her subject-matter knowledge and insights, helped me enormously to properly highlight the core of my message and gave me the confidence to know that people would really be interested to hear it.

Lidwine Holtzer, a partner at Authentiek Leiderschap B.V., for giving me detailed feedforward after every chapter, enabling me to clarify and define my message.

Milko de Kruijff, the friend with whom I spent many nights discussing – and of course solving – global problems and who, as a target audience reader, helped me to see whether things would (or would not) register with readers.

Carina Mak for her enormous drive, entrepreneurship and fun in jointly managing our company, where we work towards achieving happiness and success. *You make it happen!*

All my colleagues from Authentiek Leiderschap, who make the world a little better every day.

Richard Burton who helped me to take this book all over the world.

Fons Trompenaars for his wisdom and for creating the opportunities to enter the UK market.

All my clients for giving me the opportunity to share their insights, problems, successes, disappointments, egos and missions with me, enabling me to discover what does and does not work in practice.

All of you have helped me with my mission, and that makes me happy.

Bas W. Blekkingh
Hilversum, April 2015

Explanatory note

The original Dutch publication of this book in 2005 had quite an impact. I had not expected that individuals, teams and organisations would have such great need for our philosophy. After a successful launch, the book has become a standard work in many management and coaching courses. We started a company called Authentiek Leiderschap, guiding individuals, teams and organisations to live according to the philosophy of Authentic Leadership. This approach demonstrably increases their success and sense of fulfilment.

Authentic Leadership has since become a catchphrase. It is a form of leadership that centres on a leader's inspiring mission. Thousands of leaders and influencers have been moved by the profound and, at the same time, practical insights of our philosophy with regard to Authentic Leadership. Does this mean that it is the only truth? Of course not! But it is a way of looking at things that very quickly penetrates the surface and facilitates the development of individuals, teams and organisations.

I wrote this revised edition in 2013 on the basis of new insights gained by my colleagues at Authentiek Leiderschap B.V. and myself in practice in the Netherlands and abroad. I did not need to rectify or retract anything for this new edition as everything still appeared to be up to date. However, I did add a few new insights and approaches:

- How individuals, teams and organisations can stretch their comfort zones to gain success, self-confidence and job satisfaction.

- That you can distinguish between Comfort Zones, Growth Zones, Contraction Zones and Reckless Zones in behavioural development.

- How invisible, restricting patterns in organisations can be uncovered and made manageable.

- How restrictive norms can be turned into stimulating ones.

- How cultural development programmes *can* succeed and prevent people falling back into 'old behaviour'.

- That an ego is really a good thing to have, that it can even enhance your authenticity.

- How you can deal with the excessive ego behaviour of others.

- How you can use the technique of defining a personal mission to define the mission of a team or organisation.

I received a great deal of assistance via my Twitter account (@basblekkingh) from clients and colleagues for this revised edition, including a huge number of useful examples, suggestions and evidence from clients about how Authentic Leadership works in practice. The most common reactions were that Authentic Leadership leads to fast, profound and durable organisational development. I was slightly overwhelmed to receive these responses. Clients are our greatest source of inspiration. They are where the action is. To be able to go on a journey with them and witness their further development gives us a great sense of fulfilment.

Bas W. Blekkingh
Hilversum, April 2015

1
The environmental layer

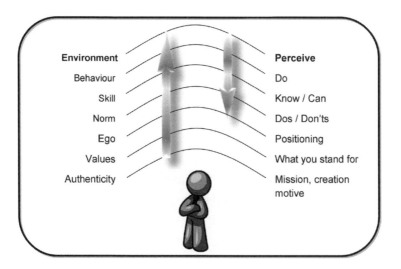

Environment	Perceive
Behaviour	Do
Skill	Know / Can
Norm	Dos / Don'ts
Ego	Positioning
Values	What you stand for
Authenticity	Mission, creation motive

As I mentioned in the Foreword, the structure of this book corresponds with the seven layers which make up all human beings. In this chapter I begin by introducing the first, outermost layer: the environmental layer. This is an important layer, since experience shows that most problems are projected onto this layer. I then explore three themes in greater detail: What does 'selective perception' mean? How do you define a problem on the environmental layer? What does selective perception mean in terms of how we communicate?

YOUR ENVIRONMENT

Imagine you're in a café getting a drink from the bar. The barman is busy so you have to wait. The person next to you (a stranger) is also waiting, so you strike up a conversation. What kinds of things do you talk about? You might tell him what part of town you live in, what line of work you're in, what your hobbies are, etc. In general, these are light topics. You will not tell him straight away that you always want to be liked, or that you think honesty is very important, or that you sometimes feel very insecure. Such topics are very likely to scare the other person off, since we are not used to broaching deep topics with strangers; we are inclined to discuss slightly 'safer' topics at a first encounter. What is striking is that these light topics are linked by a common thread: all of them say something about your environments: your residential environment, your home environment, your working environment and your recreational environment. Although you aren't saying very much about who you really are, you are saying something about how you look at these environments.

The environmental layer is an abstract concept. It is your layer, but it concerns the world around you. The environmental layer is important since most people project their problems onto this layer. They have problems with a controlling boss, for example, or a nagging neighbour, a hostile community or a declining market. Experience shows that people are quick to project their problems onto this outermost layer. You will later come to understand that this has little to do with Authentic Leadership. It is therefore worth examining this layer in greater detail.

TRY THIS...

Take off your watch without looking at it. Put it in your back pocket or somewhere else where you can't see it. If you don't wear a watch, use the clock you look at most often. Now take a piece of paper and a pen and draw what your watch looks like. You have three minutes. Draw in all the details: hands, numbers, lines, points, brand, strap, colour.

Now get your watch out and compare it with your drawing. You will probably see differences: a different brand name, Roman instead of Arabic numerals, a forgotten date display, no lines, different colour. Some people even confuse a round watch with a square one. You may of course have drawn a perfect likeness. If so, you are one of the few (or you have a very basic watch). People look at their watch on average thirty times a day. This adds up to about 11,000 times a year. Nevertheless, many people don't know exactly what their watch looks like.

SELECTIVE PERCEPTION

I chose this example because it serves as a good illustration of the simple operation of selective perception. You don't know exactly what your watch looks like because you don't think it's important. It's as simple as that. You look at your watch a lot, but the only thing you really look at is the time. This means that you look at the position of the hands or the digital numbers. The last time you really saw what your watch looks like was probably when you bought or received it. You only perceive the things in your environment that you consider important – at a particular point in time. Incidentally, 'important' does not mean 'nicest'. It only says something about what is most on your mind at that particular point in time. This is largely a subconscious process.

The following examples may sound familiar:

- You have just bought a new car. You now see the same model everywhere you look (maybe even the same colour).

- You're sitting in a café and overhear someone say your name, although you didn't follow the rest of their conversation.

- The soft ticking of an alarm clock is keeping you awake, while all you want to do is sleep.

- You can think of hundreds of reasons why something will not work.

- You can think of hundreds of reasons why something will work.

The above examples (and thousands of others) have everything to do with selective perception. If you think your new car is important, you will see it everywhere you look, since you are (subconsciously) receptive to it. Other makes are less likely to catch your eye. Because you consider your name to be very important, you catch it among all the other sounds around you. Because you are annoyed, the ticking of the alarm clock assumes such importance that it becomes a dominant noise.

For these reasons, you fail to perceive many of the things in the world around you. You are also capable of misrepresenting things in your mind. For example, think of all the things on your watch that you failed to draw and all the things you drew which are not on your watch. You made associations in your mind which do not exist in reality. You seem to have a (mental) filter that filters out any information from the world around you that you consider unimportant: *selective perception* (see Figure 1.1). This clearly shows the need to be honest and self-aware about your perception of the world around you. What is true of your perception of your watch is even more so when you are forming an opinion about someone's behaviour. It is therefore essential to realise that when you interact with others, you don't see the truth, just your version of the truth.

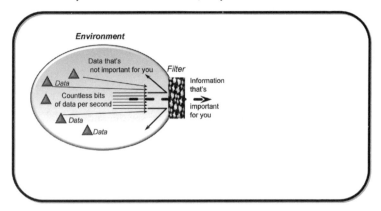

Figure 1.1 Filter operation

We use this filter because our system can't process an overload of information. Imagine having to register and store everything that happens in the world around you; it simply wouldn't be possible. A filter is a useful mechanism, however, you should be aware of its limitations. Because of it you fail to perceive many of the things that are really out there.

PROJECTING PROBLEMS ONTO THE ENVIRONMENTAL LAYER

People tend to project most of their problems onto the environmental layer. Problems that belong on the environmental layer concern a problematic environment. For example: I have a controlling boss, one of my colleagues is always complaining, my client is not paying her bills, today's youth are lazy, my neighbour is a nag, my parents have never supported me, there is famine in Sudan, the shop has sold out of cauliflower. In other words, both big and small problems can be found on the outermost layer. What they have in common is that the cause or 'fault' of the problem lies with your environment. The problem can be defined as:

My environment is the problem.

You therefore position yourself as a victim of this environment. For example: 'My boss doesn't take me seriously.' As I pointed out in the Foreword, it is important to project a problem onto the appropriate layer so that you can establish its *correct level*. With regard to problems on your environmental layer, you have to check if your perception – and the corresponding emotional response – is accurate, since you now know that your filter means that you are only receptive to things you consider important. You should therefore try to separate the things you perceive from how you label them. First, describe the facts as you perceive them in the world around you, that is, just describe what you see: my environment does this or that. In the example of the boss, this could mean that you replace 'My boss does not take me seriously,' with 'My boss never takes up my suggestions.' Then ask yourself two questions:

1. *Is that always the case?* 'Does my environment always...?' You may be oversimplifying things. In any case, try to see the nuances and re-define the problem. For example: 'My environment often...' In the example of the boss: 'My boss only takes up a few of my suggestions.'

2. *Is my judgement, or my label, correct?* 'Is it really true that my environment…?' 'Can I think or feel differently about this?' For example: 'Is it really true that my boss doesn't follow my suggestions?' 'Can I think or feel differently about this?' 'Could it actually have to do with the quality of my suggestions?'

Try to use your new insights to redefine the problem. Put the problem in the first person. We are going to make it your problem, not that of your environment. You will see that this casts your problem in a different light. For example: 'I find it annoying not to know if the environment…' or 'It bothers me that my environment…' In the example of the boss: 'It bothers me that my boss only takes up a few of my suggestions.'

So now you're at the wheel. It's no longer your environment's problem – it's *your* problem. The good thing is that you can now turn in any direction you want: you can complain or deal with a problem, or you can accept a problem, or walk away from it. It's your call, not that of your environment. You have perceived the world around you slightly more objectively and have consciously separated your perception from your emotional responses. This will enable you to work towards a better solution. In any case, it will put you in a better position to discuss a problem.

COMMUNICATION BASED ON SELECTIVE PERCEPTION

Conflicts sometimes arise because something goes wrong in the *manner of communication*. This is often because the person you're speaking to feels too little opportunity to give his opinion. Things are presented too concretely, as if they are the only truth, not just a selective perception. By really accepting that you don't determine the objective truth, and by being able to convey this to others, you enable the people around you to hold a mature dialogue. A few communication examples are given in Table 1.1.

Accept that others may hold other truths because of their filters. By understanding this, you will increase the chance of solving a problem properly. I will deal with this in greater detail in Chapter 3 when I discuss the SHAPE technique (sharing perceptions).

Table 1.1 Communication based on selective perception

It is not so	It is so
That's how it is	I think that's how it is/It's my impression that…/It would seem to me that…
You're so…	I think you're so…
That's nonsense	I think that's nonsense/I don't agree
It would be best if…	I think it would be best if…

TRY THIS…

Describe the environments you consider so important that you want to invest in them.

You spend time in different environments. To be able to translate theory into practice, it is advisable to choose three specific environments in which you would like to invest. Examples of environments include family, work and associations.

SUMMARY

The environmental layer consists of your environment as you perceive it. In other words, it is not your actual environment, since you only perceive the things that are important to you due to selective perception. Because a filter prevents an information overload, you fail to perceive many things that really exist.

You may also think that things happened in your environment that never actually took place. You are capable of misrepresenting events in your mind.

Problems that belong on the environmental layer concern a problematic environment. In practice, many people project problems onto the environmental layer and leave it at that. In doing so, they position themselves as a victim. You are therefore well advised to examine problems on the environmental layer in greater detail. You can do so by taking a careful look at the problem definition. Ask yourself if the problem could have been oversimplified, if the emotional overtones you feel are justified. Always put a problem in the first person.

When you communicate with others, try to bear in mind that what you experience is only *your* perception, not the truth.

2
The behavioural layer

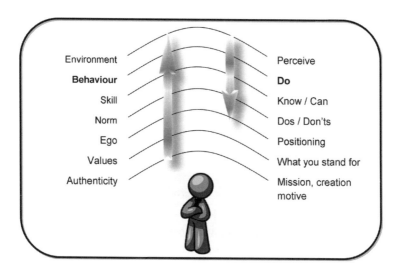

The second layer, the behavioural layer, concerns the behaviour you display in your environmental layer. I will first deal with the origins of behaviour. I then discuss the concept of the self-fulfilling prophecy. You will then discover what motives drive your behaviour and what rewards you seek. This will help you see how effective it is to have a good vision. The potential rewards of behaviour are then further elaborated. I will show that, because of all kinds of processes in your inner world, you are continually selecting the modes of behaviour from which you stand to gain the most at a particular point in time. This raises the question of your responsibility to do something about it. Finally, I will discuss the problem that belongs on this layer and the four approaches to it. You will gain new insights that will enable you to solve your problems, and those of others, more effectively.

People display different types of behaviour in their environment in order to exert influence on that environment:

- Peter has felt from an early age that it's no fun being alone. He has discovered that people respect and befriend him when he does his work better than they do. Peter works hard, very hard.

- Robert makes people laugh with his jokes.

- Hank is afraid of failure and therefore never opens his mouth.

- Jake gets his own way by dominating others.

- Anne tries to bond with others by telling them how hard she's got it.

- Joyce, the new manager, really needs recognition. She lets everyone see how good she is.

- Patrick questions his girlfriend Nancy's love for him. He often discusses this with her.

The behavioural layer is a clearly discernible layer on which you do all kinds of things: you talk, run, keep quiet, touch things. It is an important layer since it is the deepest layer that others can perceive of you. Others see, hear and feel your behaviour, selectively of course. The behaviour you display results from processes taking place inside and outside of you. Although we know a lot about the origins of behaviour, there is much more we don't know.

WHAT ARE THE ORIGINS OF BEHAVIOUR?

As we have seen, only some of the events in the world around you are allowed into your inner world. These environmental stimuli are eventually transformed into information, or stories. There are many stories in your inner world, stories which you selectively perceived at one time and which you have developed over the years. These stories represent your 'truth'. About all the things you know and are capable of; about what you think of the world; about what is right and what is wrong; about how you see yourself and how you would like to be seen by others. Stories about why you're here on earth. Every story – or combination of stories – has its own qualification, its own judgement or label: something is hot, cold, pretty, ugly, safe, unsafe.

SELF-IMAGE

Some of the most important stories in your inner world are about your self-image: the stories about yourself. Have you noticed that you hold contradictory stories about yourself? On the one hand you're independent; on the other hand you need a lot of affirmation. You sometimes don't care what others think of you. At other times you are bothered by their criticism. One moment you want to be liked, the next you bring someone down. In other words, you appear to have several self-images. Incidentally, these are not all lofty (images): respectful, ambitious, modest, dedicated. They can also be everyday images: whether or not you like sprouts, whether you can ride a bike or drive a car. Your self-image is a motley collection of stories about yourself. About how you think you behave in certain situations. About what you do, think and feel in such situations. You will learn in Chapter 5 that self-images form the basis of what we later refer to as 'the ego'.

You saw in Chapter 1 how difficult it is to describe something 'real', such as your watch. It is even more difficult, if not impossible, to describe the truth about yourself. After all, who decides what the truth is? You? But if I think differently about you, surely that's true as well? You will see that different truths about you can exist side by side.

You are always filtering in information that confirms your self-image (in both positive and negative ways) and this is essential for your further development. For example, imagine having to give a presentation in front of twenty-five people. Your self-image tells you that you are not good at giving presentations. A few things in the group will then immediately catch your attention:

- two members of the audience are checking the time (they already want to leave);

- two members of the audience are whispering to each other (they don't think it's very interesting);

- someone is looking out of the window (it's not interesting).

You simply fail to see the other twenty group members who may be listening carefully and taking notes. They are not as important to you. You only perceive what you consider to be important in your environment at a particular point in time. If you are (subconsciously) preoccupied with your inability to give presentations, your filter will be wide open to confirmation of this. You filter in information that confirms your own stories. Hence, you also filter in information that confirms your self-image.

Now let's turn things around. Imagine that you are confident of your ability to give good presentations. You will then make the following observations about the group:

- people are nodding their assent at all the conclusions you draw;

- two members of the audience are checking the time (they are sad to see that your presentation is almost over);

- two members of the audience are whispering to each other (the material you have presented prompted them to discuss a practical example);

- someone is looking out of the window (the presentation has given her something to think about).

You will see that one self-image perceives things in your environment which another self-image fails to perceive (people nodding). You will also see that both self-images perceive the same things, but with completely different emotional responses (people whispering). This is why some people regard something as an opportunity while others regard it

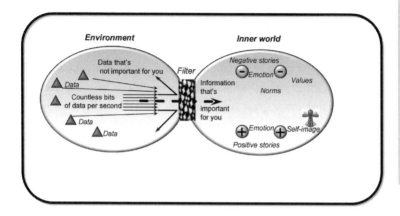

Figure 2.1 Filter, stories and self-image

as a problem. This is why some people like to take charge while others hate to do so. You either think that something suits you or not, that something fits in with your self-image or not (see Figure 2.1).

ASSOCIATION AND EVALUATION

Several processes take place in your inner world at the same time. On the one hand, your filter determines which stories it lets through and, on the other, the stories you have stored determine the openings in your filter; in other words, a chicken and egg situation. In any case, you are inclined to seek confirmation in your environment of previous stories. Of course this does not mean that you can't learn anything new; the various stories in your inner world develop at a terrific pace. Simply put: you learn faster in areas to which you – consciously and subconsciously – are more receptive. The number of stories about these themes will develop faster in your inner world than other stories. For example, someone who is interested in giving good presentations will learn good presentation skills faster than someone who is less interested in this. Associative and evaluative processes play an important role here.

You can (more or less artificially) put the processes that take place in your mind in order. This starts with certain environmental stimuli that are filtered in. This process is called *association*. When you make associations, you ask yourself where you have come across this information before. You try to link this new information to old stories, thereby giving them meaning. Environmental stimuli are eventually transformed into information. The most important stories in your inner world will have the greatest effect on this association process. If you have experienced something that left a great impression on you, this will play a major role during the association process and will eventually determine your behaviour. This is also the reason why people who have had an intense experience, for example, are sometimes no longer 'their old selves' (in a positive or negative sense).

The next process in your inner world is the *evaluation* process, when you wonder what the consequences of a perceived event are. You ask yourself 'What implications did this have for me in the past? What implications does this have for me now? How should I label this information? Does it go with my self-image? What potential consequences does this information have for me?' You could say that the most important stories are collated during the association process, and that a label is attached during the evaluation process. Something is labelled as good, nice, disgusting, attractive, painful, etc. You will then assess the potential courses of action. The courses of action from which you eventually make your choice will, by and large, have produced the best results in the past.

Only now do you come to your *mode of behaviour*. How you eventually behave will result from a process that took place in your inner world. Your behaviour is determined by *your* associations and evaluations, not by the events in the world around you. In other words: it is *you*, not the world around you, that decides on the mode of behaviour which will produce the greatest rewards for you. Thus, if someone close to you says something awful about you, *you* will decide – consciously or subconsciously – how to assess and respond to this. Behaviour is therefore a (subconscious) choice. This is *always* the case. You will always display behaviour for which you stand to gain the most at a particular point in time. Even when you do something which you know is bad for you, this is bound to be offset by a greater reward. Take smoking, for example. You know that smoking is bad for you, but still do it. For a smoker, the short-term rewards of smoking exceed the long-term rewards of giving up smoking. What complicates matters is that a 'good' reward for one person is not necessarily a 'good' reward for another (e.g. a criminal's goals are *very* different from his victim's).

Although the association and evaluation processes are portrayed here as simple, one-off, clear, steady, objective processes, many association and evaluation processes take place within a fraction of a second. In his book *Flow*, Mihaly Csikszentmihalyi discusses the quantity of information humans can handle. It appears that we can process no more than seven pieces of information (e.g. sounds, visual stimuli, recognisable nuances of emotion, thoughts) at a time. We can distinguish eighteen different sets of information per second, that is, no more than 126 per second or 7,560 per minute. That seems like a lot except that Csikszentmihalyi also states that you need forty pieces of information per second to be able to hear what someone is saying, not counting the other bits of information we register (e.g. facial expression, clothing, touch). Moreover, when you realise that speech content only accounts for 10% of influence, sound and volume 30% and non-verbal communication 60%, you will realise how difficult it is to fully understand the person you're speaking to.

You will therefore select the (mode of) behaviour which you think will produce the *greatest rewards*, that is, a mode of behaviour is selected which benefited you the most or cost you the least in the past. This process takes place during major *and* minor decision-making: when you duck an overhanging branch *and* when you buy a property. You might imagine that many associations made when buying a property are made consciously, while ducking a branch has become a learned response. But in both examples, you decide on a particular mode of behaviour having 'considered' the consequences of both events during the evaluation process. The entire process (from association and evaluation to behaviour) is represented in Figure 2.2.

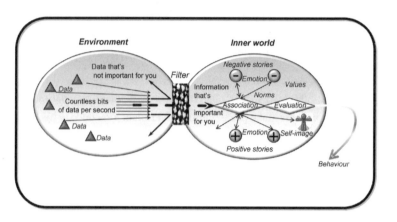

Figure 2.2 From association and evaluation to behaviour

TRY THIS...

Describe the events (e.g. a death, being fired, illness, divorce, an accident) that had such an impact on your life that they affected your behaviour at a later stage. Also consider whether this effect was a positive one.

If that was not the case, try to add nuance to the story by using the information from Chapter 1 (defining a problem on the first layer). Otherwise this story might continue to have an excessively negative effect on your further development.

Describe the various self-images you recognise in yourself: What kind of person are you? You might want to ask your partner or a good friend which of your images they recognise. It will of course be interesting to compare the differences and determine the situations/environments in which they arise (I will discuss various self-images in detail in Chapter 5).

SELF-FULFILLING PROPHECY

The behavioural examples from the beginning of this chapter are repeated below. These concern almost subconscious behaviour. I will now add a few examples of potential rewards:

• Peter has felt from an early age that it's no fun being alone. He has discovered that people respect and befriend him when he does his work better than they do. Peter works hard, very hard. His career is progressing very nicely. He is praised by his colleagues. They are happy to work with him. Now he is never alone.

• Robert makes a lot of people laugh with his jokes. This gets him the respect he longs for.

• Hank is afraid of failure, so he never opens his mouth. He therefore doesn't make any mistakes and is allowed to stay in the group.

• Jake gets his own way by dominating others. This makes others respect him and do what he wants.

• Anne often tries to bond with others by telling them how hard she's got it. She feels better when she gets support and understanding from others.

• Joyce, the new manager, really needs recognition. She lets everyone see how good she is. Everyone respects her for her achievements.

• Patrick questions his girlfriend Nancy's love for him. He often discusses this with her. By talking about it, Nancy can tell him how much she loves him, thereby removing his doubts.

Everyone in the above examples has displayed – consciously or subconsciously – behaviour that has produced a desired reward. In psychology, this process is known as a '*self-fulfilling prophecy*'. You are (sub)consciously living the story you have stored. The people in these examples want to create something and all of them accomplish the positive story they have stored in their heads. In themselves, these are logical stories. The examples are given again below, with different endings:

- Peter has felt from an early age that it's no fun being alone. He has discovered that others respect and befriend him when he does his work better than they do. Peter works hard, very hard. He surpasses everyone. Because he wants to be the best, he sees everyone else as a competitor. Others are therefore reluctant to work with him. He has complained lately of feeling increasingly lonely.

- Robert thinks he always has to be funny. He therefore becomes less fun to be around. He feels that others are not taking him seriously.

- Hank is afraid of failure, so he never opens his mouth. He therefore doesn't contribute to the group and doesn't really belong in it.

- Jake gets his own way by dominating others, and they try to thwart him in increasingly subtle ways.

- Anne often tries to bond with others by telling them how hard she's got it. The people around her think she is a moaner and drop her.

- Joyce, the new manager, has so much need for recognition that she becomes impossible to work with.

- Patrick questions his girlfriend Nancy's love for him. He discusses this with her almost every day. Nancy is increasingly annoyed with Patrick because she feels her integrity is being attacked.

These examples also reflect the phenomenon of the self-fulfilling prophecy. You ensure that the story is realised as predicted in your inner world. However, the ending turns out to be different from the one you had envisioned. This is probably because in the second example it was a negative story driving the behaviour. A self-fulfilling prophecy is an important and very complex phenomenon. It is nice when it leads to fulfilment and success, but it is very annoying when it has negative consequences. Imagine having a very negative story about something in your inner world, like Robert, who thinks he always has to be funny or else he'll be thrown out of the group. The following will then take place in your inner world:

1. You will only perceive the things in your environment which you consider important at a particular point in time. Unfortunately, 'important' does not necessarily mean that these things are pleasant or

positive, it could also be an unpleasant but relevant experience. You will therefore filter in information that conforms to this negative experience. (Once again, they're not paying any attention to me.)

2. You will use previous negative stories to make associations and evaluations. (I've been through this before. They will surely throw me out of the group.)

3. The negative story drives one's behaviour. (I've almost been thrown out of the group. I must stop this happening.)

4. Even if you start behaving differently to avoid this negative story, the image of this story will still feature prominently in the background. (I'll just play the joker. That stopped me being thrown out of the group in the past.)

5. Fear will continue to play a role in your behaviour. You will provoke the negative story by your very efforts to prevent it. (Still not expelled from the group? I'll just play the joker again.) Your filter is still wide open to information that confirms these fears. (They're already laughing less enthusiastically. Oops, this is going wrong. One more joke?)

6. Your fears will come true through your very efforts to compensate for them. (You see, they're tired of me. They're ignoring me. They're going to throw me out of the group. I knew it!).

If your fears continue to drive your behaviour, the negative self-fulfilling prophecy will cause them to come true in the long-term. You need to replace the negative story with a stronger positive one. I will elaborate this further in Chapter 5. The negative self-fulfilling prophecy is represented in Figure 2.3.

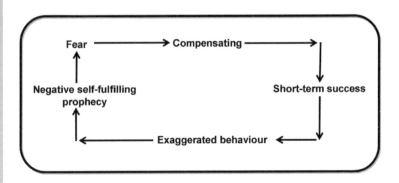

Figure 2.3 Negative self-fulfilling prophecy

It is important that you recognise a negative story about yourself and turn it into a positive one. Take your time with this. If you think you're not capable of something, think back to when certain things did work out. Try to find out why they worked out well then. Try to project these examples onto the current situation. Try to imagine that the situation you're facing is going extremely well. Try to fill your inner world with relevant positive stories. This will give you some control over your self-fulfilling prophecy. Bear in mind that this will only work if you really believe in the positive story you're thinking of. Modern techniques involving visualising something you really don't believe in simply do not work.

SELF-TALK

Self-talk is behaviour that follows on from a self-fulfilling prophecy when you tell yourself that something will or will not work (the field of neurolinguistics has delved extensively into this area). This self-talk can take place in your mind or actually be verbalised. A self-fulfilling prophecy is affected by the way you talk to yourself. If you are always telling yourself that something will not work, the 'it will not work story' becomes increasingly strong in your inner world. You will therefore filter in information that confirms this. If you persistently engage in negative self-talk, you will find that you start behaving in ways that *cause* the negative consequence. Therefore, be wary of self-talk. If you talk negatively about yourself to yourself, this can be dangerous. If you recognise this, realise that it won't help you and replace it with positive self-talk. For example, replace 'I'll never manage this' with 'I will bring out the best in myself' or 'I'll show them the best I've got'. The self-fulfilling prophecy and self-talk are shown in Figure 2.4.

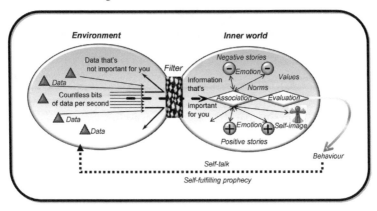

Figure 2.4 Self-fulfilling prophecy and self-talk

THINKING IN TERMS OF CONSEQUENCES

The behaviour you display comes from envisioning a particular consequence in your inner world during the evaluation process. The consequence that produces the greatest rewards will determine your choice of behaviour. Seen from this perspective, there are only two key behavioural motives: *fear* and *creation* (see Figure 2.5 for a simple representation of thinking in terms of consequences). You often see *fear* and *love* used together – perhaps an even better choice of words. However, I have noticed that many leaders are uncomfortable with the word 'love', so I use the word 'creation' in this book – fear of something and creation of something. This is not to say that fear is something akin to horror or being afraid, and that creation can only be found in great things. No, what I mean here is that fear makes you avoid a negative consequence and that creation makes you achieve a desired consequence. Both motives are rewarded, but the underlying motives differ. The insights from this section can help you enormously as an educator, manager, coach or friend.

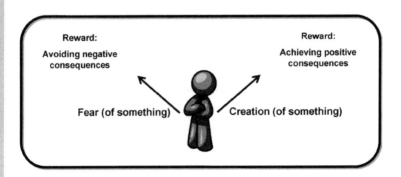

Figure 2.5 Thinking in terms of consequences: two motives

THE FEAR MOTIVE

We're sitting together in a room and I throw a poisonous snake on the floor, three metres from where you are sitting. The snake slithers towards you. What do you do? If you are not extremely fond of these reptiles *and* don't know how to deal with them, I expect you will quickly get up and rush out of the room. Why is that? You will say it was because of the snake, but that is not completely true. There is no denying the snake, but that is not what you are really afraid of. You are afraid of the *consequence* of the snake. The consequence is a painful bite, or even worse, a deadly bite. Because you don't want to be bitten, you avoid this consequence and rush from the room. You stand to gain most by leaving the room.

Incidentally, as is more often the case with fear motives, a deeper fear often drives your behaviour. For example, you might consider business to be 'not very challenging' while really you're afraid of being rejected by potential customers. With an eye on your work–life balance, you don't want to climb the management ladder, while really you're afraid of being rejected by management or fellow board members.

Back to the snake. What goes on in our inner worlds? The fact of the approaching snake is filtered in. You make associations: Where have I seen this before? In a film, in a book, in real life …? You evaluate: how will I be rewarded for this? With pain and death? What are my best options? To avoid pain or death. Your behaviour: get out!

A less extreme example is the overhanging branch. You duck because you want to avoid the negative consequence of a painful encounter with the branch. You stop for a red light because you want to avoid the consequence of a crash or a fine. You take your medication because you want to avoid the consequence of illness. Peter, from the examples given earlier, thinks he always has to be the best in order to avoid the consequence of being lonely. Robert thinks he always has to be funny because he is afraid of being excluded from the group. Hank keeps his mouth shut because he is afraid of failure. In short, fear is not the same as being afraid. This distinction is important since fear *can* be a very good counsellor.

Is fear in our genes?

This appears to be the case. Our ancestors had to continually survey their surroundings for danger. They had to be alert and able to react quickly. Danger could take them by surprise at any moment and devour them. The fact that we now predict all kinds of dangerous consequences enables us to anticipate them at an early stage.

What is good about the fear motive?

- The reward of the fear motive is that you will not die before your time and that you will be able to hold your own in unsafe environments. In this context, 'unsafe' is understood to mean 'an environment where something unwanted may happen'. You wouldn't survive a day without the fear motive (think of using the road without the fear motive).

- Fear equips you with a survival strategy and protects you from misfortune.

- Fear comprises what is called the 'push factor'; it 'pushes' you out of your current situation and may therefore lead to further development.

- The fear motive keeps you on your toes and ensures that you take immediate action: fight or flight.

- Fear makes you act faster. You simply have to, otherwise …

- The sense of relief you get when you have avoided a negative consequence, when you see that the danger is over, can be great.

Business-wise, use of the fear motive (fear of the competition, fear of
deteriorating working conditions, etc.) could have a positive, short-term
impact. Fear can create a sense of urgency for forthcoming changes.
However, when fear persists as the overriding motive it will have a para-
lysing effect. People will be truly motivated when they can work towards
a vision. This is where we speak of a creation motive, since you want to
create something. You have desires and ambitions that you want to fulfil.
Some managers know how to use the fear motive at the right time, as a
starting point, and to subsequently switch to the liberating creation motive. Thus they increase the sense of urgency in the short-term to motivate people to start acting (the push factor). Then they use the liberating
vision to motivate people to work towards a desired outcome (the pull
factor).

Business-wise, the fear motive can also have a short-term impact in that
fear unites people: us against the wicked outside world. You can see this
within families, teams, departments, organisations, cities, countries,
religions, etc. Some companies create a common enemy as a rallying
point. We have also seen many times how politicians divert attention
from dismal internal affairs by focusing attention on a common enemy.
Many demagogues were able to mobilise whole communities to keep out
'evil forces'.

What difficulties are there with the fear motive?

- It's a reactive motive.

- Your environment determines your behaviour.

- You *feel* that you have very little choice.

- Fear makes you dependent.

- It can be emotionally draining.

- Many negative feelings might arise.

- It may leave you feeling insecure.

- Fear can lead to panic, and thus poor decisions.

- Too many stressful or frightening incidents might stop you trying new things and keep you from developing further. You will simply hide in your shell.

- Your comfort zone may shrink.

- It takes a lot of energy to deal with fear.

- Fear may cause you to do only the things you *have* to do (as opposed to *want* to do). If this motive forms the basis for your behaviour for too long, something will snap inside you, you will become highly-strung or passive. This applies to individuals as well as groups. Fear is contagious, especially when expressed as a complaint.

- One fear motive often gives rise to another.

- In the long-term, the mechanism of the negative self-fulfilling prophecy leads towards the realisation of your fears.

- The leader who uses the fear motive a lot may find that it escalates out of his control. It is quite an achievement to be able to channel it successfully, and a disaster if you can't.

What are our deepest fears?

Our deepest fears are instinctive. The three main ones are:

1. Fear of death.

2. Fear of physical pain.

3. Fear of being expelled from a group (resulting in pain and death for social animals). And this is separate from the emotional pain we might feel. The fear of being expelled from a group is one of the biggest fear motives driving our behaviour (see also Chapter 5).

You will appreciate that firefighters, construction workers, soldiers and other professionals have to deal with all three of these fears on a regular basis.

You can also project your fears onto those close to you; you naturally want to keep your loved ones safe from death, physical pain and expulsion from a group.

THE CREATION MOTIVE

We're back in the room together. I tell you that there is a big surprise for you in the room next door. What do you do? You will probably get up and go next door to see what your surprise is. You long for a desired consequence. The information about the nice surprise is filtered into your inner world. You make associations: Where have I seen this before? Past surprises? You evaluate: What do I stand to gain by this? Is it nice for me? What are the potential courses of action? I can remain seated or I can act. What decision worked out the best in the past? Taking action! Your behaviour: you will do the thing by which you stand to gain the most; you will get up and go to the other room.

I have used a simple example to illustrate the simplicity of things. Your behaviour in both cases – the snake and the surprise – is identical: you leave the room. Only the motive and emotional state are (completely) different. It is much nicer to do something based on the creation motive than based on the fear motive. It is nicer to desire something than to prevent something. It is nicer to *want* to do something than to *have* to do something.

Is the creation motive in our genes?

This appears to be the case. It is our deepest motive to create things. Our species would quickly die out if the will to create (offspring) was no longer in our genetic material. The term survival of the fittest says it all: only those species that are continually able to develop will survive. All species pass on their best genetic material to their offspring. Humans are able to do so consciously by creating a story and planning for it.

What's special about human beings is that we are able to envision the consequences far into the future. We are therefore able to create grand visions and anticipate dangers early. It is one of the skills that has enabled our species to survive.

What's good about the creation motive?

- The creation motive motivates and forms the basis of a vision you want to work towards. The creation motive creates a pull factor and has a proactive effect. You are positively motivated to achieve a certain objective.

- The path to this objective is enjoyable in itself.

- The rewards of the creation motive are therefore two-fold: it is nice to work towards a goal *and* it makes you feel good when you achieve it.

- Working with a vision in mind motivates the people around you. It can mobilise forces to travel the same path. Keeping a desired consequence in mind can bring out the best in others and therefore brings people together.

- The creation motive has a long-term effect.

- Success in creation leads to a rise in self-confidence.

- It's not a matter of 'having to' but 'wanting to'.

- You use the creation motive the most when your environment feels safe. Because you then don't need to worry about any negative consequences, you will feel able to focus exclusively on the vision.

- The creation motive forms the basis for all positive creations. You create things and elevate yourself and the world around you to a higher level.

- Success resulting from the creation motive brings with it a sense of satisfaction or fulfilment, instead of just a sense of relief.

- Creation inspires creation. When the people around you see that you really act according to this motive, you will see that they too adopt this approach. In this way, you will bring out the best in a team, organisation, religion, etc. The creation motive is therefore inspiring. A successful team-building session is a good example. When the first member of a team really opens up and shows both her good and vulnerable sides, you will see that this encourages others to follow suit. In this way, the group develops a much deeper bond and commitment to jointly want to create something beautiful.

• The creation motive ensures a positive self-fulfilling prophecy.

As the person ultimately responsible, your challenge is to allow this motive to become paramount within the team's collaboration (and also, for example, in your dealings with customers and suppliers): the desire to really build something beautiful, of which all parties can be proud. You can assume that all parties will embrace this. You can judge the quality of a leader by the extent to which he allows the creation motive to drive behaviour and is able to mobilise the creation motives of the people around him. This is an important aspect of Authentic Leadership.

What is difficult about the creation motive?

It is not always easy to appreciate the immediate short-term effects. You may be so motivated by and convinced of the thing you want to create that you lose sight of the risks – you become too reckless. This may lead to disappointment. It is not always easy for leaders to hold on to the creation motive, since it is sometimes seriously put to the test; some staff members become deeply disappointed as a result of past experiences and no longer perceive their environment as safe, making them approach all positive initiatives with mistrust.

The interesting thing (as shown by the examples of the snake and surprise) is that two behaviours can be identical, while their underlying motives are different. And that a motive can be changed. However, this requires you to take a good look at yourself, so you realise that some things/activities stem from the fear motive. By now, you will also have learned that, in the case of fear, a negative self-fulfilling prophecy will not bring you any success or happiness in the long-term, while you must be careful not to become reckless if the creation motive takes over. These important themes will keep cropping up throughout this book. The different types of rewards or consequences of the motives are set out in Figure 2.6.

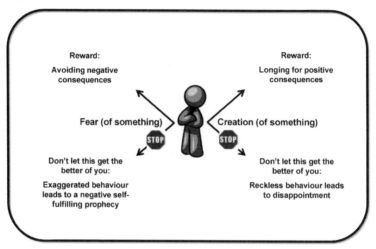

Figure 2.6   Rewards of the fear and creation motives

Some of the characteristics of the fear and creation motives are listed in Table 2.1. It is clear that both motives are necessary in one way or another. They seem to share the same source: the will to live. If you want to advance to a level where you want your creation motive to drive your behaviour, it is important to first examine your fear motives, since the things you don't want say a lot about the things you do want. The trick of Authentic Leadership is to recognise your fear motives and turn them into creation motives. An authentic leader is familiar with his fear motive, but allows himself to be driven by his creation motive since this brings out the best in himself and others and combines success with a greater sense of fulfilment.

Table 2.1 Characteristics of the fear and creation motives

Fear	Creation
Avoid negative consequences	Realise positive consequences
Push factor	Pull factor
Fear protects you from misfortune	Creation leads you to a sense of fulfilment
Reactive	Proactive
'Having to'	'Wanting to'
You are driven by external forces	You are driven by internal forces
Is used in unsafe environments (something bad might happen)	Is used in safe environments (I can be myself)
Dependent	Independent
Has an immediate effect	Is lasting
Has a short-term effect	Has a long-term effect
Makes you alert	Motivates you in a positive way
You feel good when you achieve the end result	You feel good while carrying out an activity
Infects others	Inspires others
Its contagion may result in panic or apathy	Its contagion may blind you to things
As a management style, this requires a great deal of control	As a management style, this does not require much control
Able to mobilise the effective evil of humans	Able to mobilise the effective goodness of humans

TRY THIS...

Try to discover what your fear motives are. What negative consequences are you trying to avoid? What are you really afraid of?
Are you afraid of dying, failing, of not being thought of as the
best? Carry out a self-examination. When you have discovered
your fear motives, you will be able to explain your behaviour and
emotional responses in a variety of situations. You should realise
that fears are a fact of life; they are useful, but you should also be
able to put them into perspective. You cannot directly overcome
all fears and there is no reason to. Fear motives can benefit you.
By understanding your fear motives, you will be more inclined
to accept them and might let them become less powerful – if
you choose to do so. One fear might be hiding a deeper fear. It
helps in this self-examination to keep asking yourself: 'Why is
that bad?'. For example: I'm afraid of failure. Why is that bad?
Because the people around me will no longer respect me. Why
is that bad? Because I will be cut down to size. Why is that bad?
Because people will think I'm useless. Why is that bad? They will
expel me from the group. You may have uncovered a deeper fear
here: the fear of being expelled from a group, or the fear of no
longer making a difference (incidentally, this fear often lies behind other fears).

Incidentally, in my practice I have learned that, deep inside, many managers are afraid of having their shortcomings – which they have recognised
in themselves – exposed. A closer examination has revealed that, like all
managers, they sometimes follow their instincts, making many decisions
'by the seat of their pants'. Instead of seeing this as a strength they fear
being found out. In the next section you will examine the creation motives that can help you to deal with these fears.

VISION

Creating a vision helps to turn a fear motive into a creation motive. I use the word 'vision' to mean: *an image of a desired future*. You can create a vision about any subject, whether it be a future sketch of your company or your family composition. You portray your environment or yourself as you wish it to be. The power of a good vision is that it makes people more effective. People with a vision have a clear motivation and a sense of the direction they wish to take, because they are driven by the creation motive. In a variety of situations, the vision can be a beacon on which to focus behaviour. It would be interesting to explain this using the themes discussed in this chapter. If you have developed a strong vision, this means it has been stored in your inner world as an important story. A strong vision changes your perception of your environment. You will filter in information that is important for your vision. This does not require any extra effort (see Figure 2.7). Provided that you think of your vision as realistic you should, as it were, really be able to live it. When you close your eyes, you should be able to describe what you see, hear, feel and, possibly, smell and taste. You should be able to describe your behaviour at that particular point in the future (see also Chapter 7).

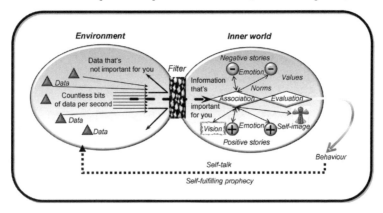

Figure 2.7 Vision in the inner world

As a leader, it is a challenge to create a vision *and* share it with others. If others adopt your vision, they too will become more effective through selective perception. To realise this, it will not be sufficient to share your vision a couple of times and prepare a document or presentation about it. No, you will have to take your associates on an imaginary journey to this future situation several times. Think of a way to firmly establish the vision as a strong story in their inner worlds. Let them 'live' it as if it has already been realised. The example of Martin Luther King has inspired many leaders to approach their colleagues with an 'I have a dream' narrative (whereby the dream is presented as a modern-day truth). Some companies have produced a 'newspaper', dated five years in the future, containing articles, interviews and adverts that portray the vision. Use your creativity or hire creatives. Present your vision as if it were today's reality.

Is a vision an end in itself or a means to an end?

At first glance a vision appears to be an objective. You talk about an image of a desired future, a kind of end-game. At a higher level of abstraction, you see that having a vision is a means to an end. It enables you to effectively make use of the way you behave in the here and now. It focuses your activities. You could therefore say that a vision is a means to an end, intended to make your behaviour more effective and lead to a wished-for, positive self-fulfilling prophecy. The good thing is that every step that brings you closer to your vision is a joy in itself. The journey is as rewarding as the destination. Treat yourself to such a journey and develop visions about environments you wish to invest in. A vision will allow you to let your creation motive lead the way, with all the associated benefits.

TRY THIS...

Think back to Chapter 1 and the exercise in which you described the environments you would like to invest in. Take your time to develop a vision of each environment. Answer the following question: what will this environment look like in five years' time if everything works out the way I want? The second clause is particularly important. Assume that everything works out; don't let yourself be held back by just focusing on the impossibilities.

Now try to turn your fear motive into a creation motive. Instead of 'preventing something', look for 'something to create, something you want to achieve'. Create a vision in which fear no longer plays a role. You can do this by describing the (positive) opposite of your fear. For example, 'fear of death' becomes 'enjoy every day', 'failure' becomes 'give it a chance to succeed'. Another example which will be recognised by many managers is the fear of not being thought of as the best; that is why they want to be 'the best'. Managers who want to be the best make themselves dependent on their rivals. If a competitor scores a six, the best will need to score a seven; if a competitor scores an eight, the best will have to score a nine. Such constant comparison is exhausting. A good alternative is to aim to 'bring out the best in yourself'. This will put the ball in your court, and your rival's score won't matter so much.

If you are confronted by a fear (e.g. not being the best), you can consider the following courses of action:

- Make light of the fear when you recognise it (It's him again).

- Ask yourself if your fear is justified (Will I really be thrown out if I'm not the best?). If it's not true, your fear will largely disappear.

- Try to find out what the rewards of your fear are, what you stand to gain by it (I won't be expelled from the group).

- Then try to find out what the rewards of the alternative creation motive are (I'm giving them the best I've got. There's nothing more I can do).

- Now select which motive you want to lead the way and behave accordingly (If I give the best I've got and focus on that, the best results will automatically follow. In any case, they'll certainly want to keep me in the group).

BEHAVIOURAL REWARDS

You have already seen that your behaviour is determined by the story that produces the greatest rewards. You behave according to what you stand to gain. You want (often subconsciously) to realise or avoid a certain consequence. If you want to change your behaviour in certain environments, it is important to find out what rewards steer or drive your behaviour. Below you will find various rewards that could be the basic motive for your behaviour.

Staying alive (don't die)

This is the reason we stop for a red light and don't climb over the fence in a zoo to see whether crocodiles are really as fast as people say. This is also why many people avoid getting involved in a fight. Conversely, it is what moves some people to live life on the edge; they want to feel the thrill of being alive (e.g. bungee jumping and parachuting).

Avoiding physical pain

Not being in pain is often a reward for our behaviour. This is why we are generally careful. This is what we try to teach our children from an early age. People who have experienced pain are more likely to seek this reward. Simple examples: wearing shin-guards in football and a helmet on a motor bike.

Seeking sensory stimulation

In contrast with 'avoiding physical pain', we often seek out positive stimuli, such as a good feeling, taste or smell, or seeing or hearing something beautiful. It is the reward that motivates you to go to the hairdresser, or to a good concert. It is why you want to have a good meal, or put on a nice perfume.

Being right

I mention this separately because it is an important reward, even though it can obstruct your further development. You sometimes think it's more important to be proved right that you are not something than to receive confirmation that you are. This is largely a hindrance for people with a negative self-image. They are (subconsciously) trying to prove, via a negative self-fulfilling prophecy, that they are not cut out for something. When this is finally shown to be the case, they seem to be overcome with relief ('I told you I couldn't do it'). Being proved right justifies not having to try again. Even if something does work out, you might put it down to chance, since 'I'd rather be right about being unable to do something so I can stop trying' than 'run the risk of failure when trying'.

Financial security

Money is important. It allows you to buy beautiful, enjoyable and useful things for yourself and others. It is also one of the reasons you work. Perhaps it's also one of the reasons not to correct your boss (when you could well do so): it could have financial consequences. In my practice I have found that people sometimes exaggerate financial consequences. When you actually lay out the consequences in concrete terms (e.g. by describing a worst-case scenario should you be fired), finances hardly appear to play a role at all. People usually manage for a while, until they find a new job. The same is true of many people who want to strike out on their own but are afraid to do so because of the financial risks involved. Here too we see that these fears can be dismissed if we put them in concrete terms.

Pursuing instant gratification

This is a 'tricky' reward since it's difficult to recognise. We are sometimes driven by instant gratification, although we know this may result in a more negative reward in the longer term. Take smoking, for example. Everyone knows that smoking is unhealthy, but giving up doesn't produce immediate results. This also applies to people who want to lose weight; eating fatty or sugary foods provides instant gratification, while losing weight doesn't provide rewards until much later. Another example is that we're not always prepared to confront others directly about improving their behaviour in the long-term as we gain less from this than from maintaining a good relationship in the short-term.

Feeling recognised: receiving confirmation that you make a difference

This is the deepest mental reward you strive for, consciously but mostly subconsciously. It touches on the core message of this book. You want to receive confirmation that your life has meaning. This 'proof' can be obtained in two different ways.

In the first place, your creation. You are a creative being. You create all kinds of things, for yourself and for others. If the human species didn't have this motive, it would probably have died out a long time ago. Seeing your final creation proves that you exist, that you make a difference. That is a nice feeling. If you hadn't been around, your creation would never have been realised. Having children is a good example of creation that you are reminded of every day. Other examples include writing a book, painting a picture, setting up a company and helping the people around you to develop further.

Creating is a way to have your 'being' here on earth confirmed. Being and creation are therefore two concepts that go hand-in-hand. A creation is tangible proof of your existence. You recognise your 'being' in your creation: Creating $\approx$ Being.

The trick is to be conscious of the things you want to create. You can develop this skill. You can rise to a level where you are continually aware of the things you want to create. This is another way of saying that your creation motive leads the way. Why should that be so? Because it is so rewarding. It gives you a sense of fulfilment when you try to define yourself through something you create. The question of why this makes us feel so good has preoccupied me for a long time. What else makes us feel good? You could think, for example, of eating, drinking and sex. Apparently we need all of these to continue to exist, and they reward our body and soul with a good feeling. After all, it would be difficult to have to eat regularly, let alone have sex, if these were not pleasurable activities. Evolution has probably made sure that the human species is rewarded for behaviour that guarantees its continued existence. This may also be the case with the good feeling you get when you create something. By creating, we guarantee the continued existence of our kind. Because it feels good to be rewarded, humans are stimulated to pass on, in whatever shape or form, the best they have got to give to others. Practice has shown that people experience the greatest sense of fulfilment when they realise a desired creation. They wouldn't do this if they didn't feel safe in their environment. They would otherwise have to put most of their energy into 'staying alive'.

The moral of this story is that creating rewards you with the good feeling that 'you make a difference'. This is your deepest motive. It is perhaps your deepest subconscious motive to give life the best of your life. Authentic Leadership is the ability to lead yourself and others according to this creation motive. Your reward is the enjoyment of the creation process as well as the enjoyment of the creation itself. In combination these give you a sense of fulfilment.

The second way to realise the reward that 'you make a difference' is to receive recognition from the people around you. The people around you can show that you make a difference. They may respect, reward, acknowledge, involve, comfort you, etc. This makes you feel accepted by a group. This makes you feel secure. You often consider (subconsciously) whether a certain behaviour will strengthen your position in a group, or whether you wish to maintain your position. The reward of 'not being expelled from the group' determines the behaviour of a lot of people a lot of the time, without them necessarily being aware of it. Questions that preoccupy us in this respect are:

- Am I good enough?

- Am I independent enough?

- Am I innocent?

- Will I be pitied?

- Will I fail?

- Am I nice, attractive, funny enough?

- Am I still the best?

- Do I help enough?

- Am I strong enough?

These rewards are discussed in detail in Chapters 5 and 7. Most people can't 'make a difference through creation' until they have 'made a difference through recognition'. Because of their need for recognition, people risk being untrue to themselves, acting in a way that has little to do with authenticity. Making a difference through creation forms the basis for Authentic Leadership.

HOW CAN YOU PUT THIS INFORMATION TO GOOD USE?

You might conclude that people act in a certain way because it leads to a desired reward: preventing something or desiring something. Therefore, even when you behave very oddly, this is bound to be rewarded somehow. You could say that a child who lies screaming on the supermarket floor is behaving rather oddly. The reward could be either positive or negative attention. A manager who continually puts other people down might want to be respected as a reward, or to avoid not being respected. Incidentally, excessive behaviour is more often driven by fear motives. If you desperately cling to undesirable behaviour, while you know how you would really like to behave, you would be well advised to first examine the rewards of the fear motive. Determine what it is you are trying to avoid and accept that this is a reward you can always fall back on. This facilitates the switch to creation-driven behaviour. This also applies to the people you manage. If they know how they would like to behave (e.g. to move more towards centre-stage) but fail to do so, you will know that their fear motive generates a better reward. When you know what the rewards are, and can control this, you will control your behaviour. You will only be prepared to change your behaviour if the rewards of an alternative behaviour are greater, therefore, try to work out what rewards you are going for. The moral of the story is that *by understanding the reward you will understand the behaviour and will develop it more easily.*

It is nice to know that fear and creation do not go hand in hand, but that one follows from the other. The creation motive is invariably your deepest motive. This doesn't mean it is always visible; it could be concealed by a fear motive. Fear ensures that the creation is protected. Because of your fear of rejection, you won't immediately bare your soul or share your deepest creation motives when you meet someone for the first time. However, your (possibly) reserved behaviour doesn't mean you don't have a soul. All fear-driven behaviour conceals a creation you want to protect.

FEAR PROTECTS CREATION

This means that a person's fear-driven behaviour could serve to protect a valuable creation, although the person may not be aware of this. Can you, as an authentic leader, still spot the beautiful creation behind the fear-driven behaviour of others? This starts with the belief that it is there.

TRY THIS...

- Which rewards drive your behaviour the most?

- What rewards would you like to drive your behaviour?

- What behaviour do you keep displaying, when you would really like to do something else? How is this behaviour rewarded/what negative consequences do you wish to avoid by behaving in this way?

Do this exercise with people you influence and who are open to influence. Also, try to guess the creation motives that underlie the strange, fear-driven behaviour of the people you have problems with.

BLAME AND RESPONSIBILITY

My boss is controlling; one of my colleagues is always complaining; my
current job does not offer good enough career prospects; I've always got
to do everything myself; my client is not paying her bills; the youth of
today are lazy; my neighbour is a nag; Sudan has been struck by famine
again; my partner has left me; being raped has ruined my life; cauliflower
is sold out. In each of these cases you can ask yourself two questions: (1)
Am I responsible for this? (2) If so, on what grounds?

TRY THIS...

Make a list of any problems that have occurred in your environment. Tick the problems you're already dealing with.

Then ask yourself why you haven't dealt with some of the other
problems.

Do you see any problems that you're not dealing with but for which you
feel responsible?

It is not my intention to make you feel responsible for everything. However, it is my intention to give you tips on how to do something about
problems in your environment. It is not always easy to determine where
your responsibility starts and ends. Moreover, 'responsibility' is a catch-
all term.

Are you responsible for the things that happen to you? On the one hand,
you have seen how you provoke things through a self-fulfilling prophecy,
although you're not immediately aware of this. You are therefore responsible for the things that happen to you. On the other hand, things happened that you weren't able to predict or control. You can ask whether
you can be held responsible for these.

Can you be held responsible for the things that were within your control
but where you weren't aware of the consequences? For example, if you

tell a tired colleague to go home early to have a good rest and the person in question is hit by a bus on the way home, are you responsible for this? Are you to blame?

Can you be held responsible for something: (1) that was within your control, (2) *and* where you considered the consequences, (3) *and* after careful consideration made a decision, (4) *which*, as it turns out, led to an awful consequence? For example, you send your daughter to school by herself for the first time, knowing that she has to cross a busy road, knowing that she has often done this quite well when you were watching her, but this time she has a minor accident. Are you responsible for this? Are you to blame?

You will have noticed that the words 'blame' and 'responsibility' are often used interchangeably. It is important to make a *distinction* between 'blame' and 'responsibility' from now on, since you can carry on feeling guilty for too long. 'Blame' says something about the past, 'responsibility' says something about the present and future. If something happened in the past which was your fault, it is your responsibility to draw lessons from this for the future. You might then be able to make up for the negative consequences of a past decision (or to prevent them from recurring). It is better to replace 'guilt that weighs heavily on your shoulders' with 'the responsibility to do things differently now and in the future'. Otherwise you will waste away, and there is no need for that since you can't change the past.

TRY THIS...

Check whether you still feel guilty about certain things. Reformulate this guilt into responsibility.

PROJECTING PROBLEMS ONTO THE BEHAVIOURAL LAYER

This book deals with the here and now and the future. It deals with the responsibility for decisions you have made and will make. Unpleasant things sometimes happen. Moreover, things happen that are not your responsibility, but for which others are to blame. The question is: Where does your responsibility start? Although you are not always responsible for the things that happen to you, you are always responsible for the decisions you make about what you want to do about a situation. And that's exactly the kind of problem that belongs on the behavioural layer.

The problem defined in Chapter 1 was:

- My environment is the problem (environmental layer).

The problem changes on the behavioural layer. The behavioural layer is where you do things. Instead of 'my environment is the problem', the problem is redefined as:

What should I do to solve my problem with my environment? What should I do to feel happy again?

Once again you are responsible for what you want to do about a problem, regardless of whether you were responsible for creating it. There are four different options, so you have your choices cut out for you: (1) complain, (2) act, (3) lower your expectations, (4) leave (you can use the mnemonic CALL). When you choose one of these four options you will be responsible for the positive and negative consequences. It is therefore a good idea to examine these four options in greater detail. Once you have analysed the consequences, you can make a *cost-benefit analysis* for yourself and make a decision regarding any problem.

FOUR APPROACHES TO A PROBLEM

Complain about the environment

Examples of complaints:

- My boss creates an unpleasant atmosphere in the department.

- One of my colleagues is always complaining.

- My neighbourhood is always a mess.

- Market demand has decreased.

- I never received compliments from my parents.

- I always have to do everything myself.

- My staff members are not good enough.

- Sudan has been struck by famine again.

- My current job does not offer good enough career prospects.

The above examples qualify as complaints if you don't do anything about them. Complaining goes beyond grumbling about a situation. What I mean by complaining is that you project the solution for the problem onto your outermost layer. You see a problem in your environment but then don't take any action. A few characteristics of complaining: (1) the environment is responsible, (2) there's nothing I can or will do about it, (3) I'm a victim, (4) I have to ..., (5) I'm not responsible. Why are you complaining? It sometimes feels good to let off steam. This is mainly because, by complaining, you are trying to imply you are not guilty. By complaining, you hope that other people will feel sympathy or won't hold you responsible for the event or solution. By complaining, you are really trying to secure your position in the group. Unfortunately, the decision to complain is in most people a subconscious one. If you really want to complain about a problem, do so consciously. And if you consciously want to complain, it is useful to know what the consequences will be.

Advantages of complaining:

- Allows you to air your feelings. This can make you feel better. A trouble shared is a trouble halved. It may even feel good to complain.

- Proving your innocence (it wasn't your fault). An advantage of complaining is that other people might not hold you responsible for the situation or expect you to assume responsibility to do something about it. You're hurting and you get sympathy. You're looking for support.

- 'Us against them' sentiment: complaining unites people. When you talk to someone who also doesn't want to be responsible for solving the problem, you will notice that (s)he will gladly back you up.

- There is no responsibility for making an effort, and it is easy to do.

- No chance of failure: by not doing anything, you won't risk your actions coming to nothing.

- Complaining won't harm the relationship in the short-term. However, a complaint about somebody always carries the risk that the relationship will deteriorate. This could happen especially if you don't have the skills to properly discuss a complaint.

Disadvantages of complaining:

- Your situation won't change. The problem won't go away. You won't solve anything.

- By definition, complaining means making yourself dependent on the people around you. The people around you determine how you feel. You position yourself as a victim.

- Be aware of negative influences. Complaining is contagious. Complaining arises from the fear motive. You want to prevent something happening, since people don't like to be held responsible for an unpleasant situation. If you give them the opportunity to back out of their responsibility, they will be only too happy to agree with you. A complaint can be used several times. Who isn't familiar with a department where everybody moans? Where every opportunity is seized to resurrect old complaints. Meanwhile, nothing is done to improve the situation.

- The problem is magnified through selective perception. This is a major risk. If you often have to deal with complaints, this 'story' will become increasingly important in your inner world. This will result in your filter increasingly letting in the necessary 'proof' from your environment.

- Positive things are interpreted negatively. For example, if a good initiative is taken to relieve the (complaint of) 'workload', the reaction could be 'they're only giving us more work'.

- Complaining results in a negative self-fulfilling prophecy. Because of an increasingly negative perception of your environment, you as a complainer will behave in a way that provokes other complaints. For example, if you don't trust a colleague, you won't involve her as much in your work. As a result, she will be suspicious of you. In turn, you will interpret her behaviour as proof that she can't be trusted.

- Your own energy levels will decrease. Complaining is exhausting. This is because only the negative aspects are highlighted. You will be overcome with a feeling of powerlessness and weariness. Stress often stems from this feeling of powerlessness as a result of 'contagious' complaint behaviour.

- The energy levels of other people will decrease. Realise that your complaints have the same effect on others. They seem to provide short-term relief, but when you take stock, complaining takes a disproportionate amount of energy out of others.

- Your reputation is damaged. People would rather not associate with complainers in the long-term, even though they will briefly back you up. They feel their energy begin to dissipate when you start complaining again. People start to avoid you as a result (Here comes that moaner). Your reputation will also be damaged if someone finds out that you're complaining or gossiping about him/her.

- Your self-image is damaged. You will not pass your own authenticity assessment (this theme is discussed in Chapter 7). You should take a good look at yourself in the mirror and ask yourself 'Is this really me? Am I someone who complains and doesn't do anything about it?' Nine times out of ten you will conclude that you should stop playing the victim.

If there is a lot of complaining in your environment (e.g. your team or company), this will drain energy from all the staff. You might nevertheless conclude that it's necessary to have complaining. So don't forbid it, since that won't work. Make the following agreement or set the following norm instead: *You can only complain if you announce your intention to complain in advance.*

This agreement will ensure that colleagues complain consciously rather than subconsciously, so they won't automatically complain, but will *choose* to complain. Another advantage is that, by mentioning it, they will manage the expectations of the person they're complaining to, since he won't have to do anything about it. It is enough to listen with genuine interest and show understanding. Many complaining colleagues are not looking for a solution. Sometimes, complaining is simply a way to evoke sympathy. As a leader, you sometimes have to offer a shoulder to lean on, to say you think it's commendable that people carry on under these extreme circumstances. In so doing, you will save an enormous amount of time and energy.

Conclusion

It is okay to complain. But, if you must complain, do so consciously. This means that you balance the pros and cons against each other. If you choose to complain, you will be responsible for the favourable and adverse consequences.

Don't complain for too long; don't go on and on about something. If you still want to complain to someone, start off by saying that you just want to let off steam. In doing so, you will manage the other person's expectations. Then focus on the things you want to deal with.

TRY THIS...

Try keeping track of the number of times you and others complain during a day. You will be amazed.

Try to think about whether the word you keep using in a certain context really means what you are saying. Does 'have to' really mean 'have to'? Or could you choose not to do something, whatever the consequences? If you have to be on time for an appointment, surely this means that you want to be on time? If so, simply use the words 'want to' instead of 'have to'. You will see that this comes across more strongly, since the responsibility for a decision is placed within yourself. And it simply feels nicer to be in control.

Act to change the environment

If you want to stop complaining about your environment, you can choose to deal with it (the rest of this book will largely address this choice). This means that you will actively start targeting your behaviour towards your environment in order to influence it. There are advantages and disadvantages to this approach.

Advantages of acting:

- Your problem might be solved.

- Your self-esteem will increase enormously.

- There is a chance that relationships will improve. If you have shown that you can discuss difficult issues with others, this means that these relationships can take a knock. Investing in a relationship means you consider working together important.

- You become less dependent on others. You take responsibility for solving the problem yourself.

- You increase your level of influence since you show the people around you that you're not afraid to deal with problems.

- You increase your chances of feeling happier again.

- You have a positive influence on and increased credibility with others: you're an example to others because you don't give up. People generally admire those who aren't afraid of dealing with problems.

- You see things more positively: you store the effective handling of a problem in your inner world as an important story. If similar problems occur in the future, you will filter in opportunities rather than limitations.

- You create a positive self-fulfilling prophecy.

- Your energy levels increase: investing in your environment and seeing that your environment is developing is one of the biggest generators of energy and happiness. You saw previously that this is one of the most important rewards determining your behaviour. Creating inspires the people around you, since one creation motive inspires another. You receive confirmation that you make a difference.

Disadvantages of acting:

- Risk of failure: you might not be able to deal with a problem successfully, or you might cause the problem to escalate. This is largely to do with not having the right skills. You might damage your image as a result.

- Takes time and energy: your focus on the problem reduces time for other activities. Ask yourself if the problem in your environment is worth investing time and energy in. A complaint will sometimes simply remain a complaint. People who are always really busy can ask themselves if they are addressing the really important issues, if perhaps they're setting the wrong priorities.

In short, dealing with a problem is an active choice, in which you take on a lot of responsibility. I discuss the most important skills you might require here in Chapter 3.

Accepting an environment by lowering your expectations

Imagine that you don't want to complain about or act to change your environment. You may then choose to accept your environment. This option is often passed over by leaders since it seems like giving up. This is why you can't accept something until you have dealt with it or thought about it. Acceptance means that you lower your expectations. You can use the happiness equation here: *Happiness: E = R (Expectations = Reality).*

$E = R$
Expectations are the stories in your head in which you describe what your environment looks like in an ideal world. Reality is the situation in

your environment as you now (selectively) perceive it. If your expectations match reality, you will feel quite satisfied or happy. For example, I expect my board of directors to stimulate me. If the board of directors actually does stimulate you, this is reflected in the following equation: $E = R$. This makes you feel comfortable.

$E < R$

Your expectations are lower than your perceived reality. This is a good thing, creating a relatively good feeling. However, you do run a slight risk of becoming complacent since you don't have any reason to take action. For example, you expect a customer satisfaction score of 7.3. An assessment shows that the score is actually 7.8, so you won't put in any more effort; things are fine as they are. You could consider raising your expectations: What can we do to increase the score to 8.3?

$E > R$

In this case, your perceived reality falls short of your expectations. This is usually not a problem. It may even be necessary, since it will make you take action to bring reality in line with your expectations (so that $E = R$). Objectives are set and visions are created in this way. An objective works like an expectation. This works in complex cases, such as a board of directors not performing adequately when you have constructive discussions to stimulate them to meet your expectations. However, it also works in a simple example, such as buying groceries. You anticipate eating cauliflower. However, you're actually out of cauliflower so you have to go out and buy some ($E = R$). Working towards a feasible result also gives you a relatively good feeling, let alone achieving the result. The more challenging an objective, the greater the level of satisfaction.

$E >> R$

In this case, reality falls significantly short of your expectations. This will cause problems. You will usually first try to do something about this reality by working harder and more effectively. However, if the situation persists for too long, you will become highly-strung. You will start to feel unhappy. It is a source of stress. I have met a lot of people in practice who have tried for too long to match reality with the high expectations they have set for themselves. Incidentally, these expectations are often expectations which they let other people put on them. It results in complaints, feelings of powerlessness, panic and stress.

You can now see the opportunities created by accepting a problem, namely, that it is not always necessary to change reality to adjust the equation from E >> R to E = R, that you can also lower your expectations. Lowering your expectations may feel unnatural, because your inclination is to do more, to manipulate reality. In some cases, it is actually wise not to do so. By accepting, you take your environment for what it is, including the disadvantages.

What are the good reasons for lowering your expectations?
An important reason for accepting the way things are, is that you can't influence the environment if a problem has occurred in it. You can worry about the current famine in Sudan, but can you exert any influence on the situation? If you think not, accept the problem and focus on other things. Another example: imagine you've got a problem with the way your parents raised you. Ask yourself if you can do anything about that now. If you can't, adjust your expectations and focus on things you *can* influence (e.g. strengthening the relationship with your parents).

Another reason to settle for acceptance is that you might be able to exert some influence, but you choose not to. You'd rather focus your energy on other things; you set other priorities. This is a conscious process: you choose to let certain things go, and therefore 'choose' the consequences of your choice. In any case, you stop complaining. Taking the example of famine in Sudan, this would mean that there are ways in which you could make a difference (e.g. by donating money, doing volunteer work), but you *choose* not to expect this of yourself. So you then lower your expectations. It is also useful to summarise the consequences of acceptance.

Advantages of accepting an environment:

- Your problem could be solved by increasingly filtering in positive things from your environment.

- You become less dependent on the problem in your environment.

- You are more likely to feel happy again, since the problem doesn't bother you as much.

- There is a reduced chance of negative influences.

- You see things more positively.

- Your credibility will not be so compromised.

- You will increase your self-esteem.

- You will refocus on things which can make you feel good.

- There is less chance of a negative self-fulfilling prophecy.

- You will not waste as much energy.

- You will eventually be proud that you didn't continue to play the victim.

Disadvantages of accepting an environment:

- Nothing changes. Even though the problem doesn't bother you as much, it is still there.

- The unpleasant feelings will not go away immediately. If you decide to stop complaining, you won't find this easy straight away.

- You may be tempted to complain.

- Some reputational damage: because you're not dealing with the problem, others might think you've taken the easy way out.

Conclusion

If you can't deal with a problem successfully, you can stop yourself falling back into complaint behaviour by accepting your environment as it is and adjusting your expectations. Decide if you can or want to deal with the problem. If not, you can make a conscious decision to accept it. If that's your choice, you'll have to put up with both its positive and negative consequences.

TRY THIS...

This week, see if you can help two complainers in your environment accept a situation by adjusting their expectations.

Leave an environment

You might choose to leave an environment which is giving you problems. You want to stop complaining but don't want to act on or accept the environment. Leaving could mean that you focus your energies on other things in the same environment, but it could also mean that you physically move to another environment (e.g. another department, another company, another city, another country, another partner). In general, this is a major decision. It is important to list the pros and cons here.

Advantages of leaving an environment:

- You won't be faced with the problem in your environment any more.

- Your self-esteem will increase; you have taken action. You can be proud of yourself for no longer complaining about your problems, but having actually taken some initiative.

- You will increase your credibility with the people around you. You're an example of someone who doesn't sit back but actively looks for other options.

- New environment, new opportunities.

Disadvantages of leaving an environment:

- You have thrown out the good with the bad. By leaving the environment you have problems with, you also leave behind the good things it had to offer. For example, looking for another job means that you give up old certainties (nice colleagues, good fringe benefits, etc.).

- You will have to get used to and adapt to a new environment and settle into your new job.

- The problem may (re)occur in your new surroundings (as a result of your perception and a negative self-fulfilling prophecy). You have been exposed to certain images that annoyed you for a long time and this story (although not a very nice one) has thus become very important in your inner world. You therefore (subconsciously) filter in situations that resemble the old story. As a result, you might be more inclined to see problems that remind you of the situation in your old environment.

- You may feel like you've 'run away'. If this persists, you will regard leaving as a cowardly deed (although this need not necessarily be the case). Therefore, when you walk away from a problem try to focus on the challenges your new surroundings have to offer. Close the chapter and open a new one. When you walk away, you choose a new environment.

CALL is a simple mnemonic that you can immediately put into practice. If someone comes to you with a problem, first ask her what she wants to do about it: just get something off her chest (Complain), get help to find a solution (Act), accept (Lower expectations) or move to another environment (Leave). The person may look at you a little strangely after these questions. She will then very likely make it clear that she just wanted to get something off her chest. That's fine. This means that you, and others, won't have to spend a lot of time on less important activities. If you can keep this up consistently, the people around you will learn to think in terms of CALL before they step into your office.

TRY THIS…

Think about the problems presented at the beginning of this section and decide on a course of action for each problem: complain, act, lower expectations or leave.

SUMMARY

You can divide the world in two: the world around you and the inner world you create in your mind. You have stored all kinds of past experiences in your inner world as stories. Every story has its own emotional charge or label: good, cold, safe, etc. Your experience in dealing with a variety of situations has gone into creating a certain story about yourself, i.e. your self-image. You have various self-images stored in your inner world.

The more important a story is for you, the more you will filter in information related to the story. Once information has been filtered in, a number of processes will take place. First of all, you make associations: you ask yourself where you have come across this before. You will evaluate all these stories once you have collated them. After this evaluation, you will eventually choose to behave in a way that produces the greatest rewards. The entire process takes place in fractions of seconds, largely without you being aware of it.

You seek rewards, consciously and subconsciously, through your behaviour: staying alive, avoiding physical pain, gaining sensory stimulation, being right, financial security, immediate gratification, proving that you make a difference. Proof that you make a difference can be obtained in two different ways. In the first place, you can claim a certain position in the world around you (this reward forms the basis for your ego layer). In the second place, you can create something in your environment by giving the best you've got; when you see this creation, it will give you the good feeling that you make a difference (this reward forms the basis for your authenticity layer). If you want to change your behaviour, it is important to first understand the rewards of your old behaviour, since you won't change your behaviour until you stand to gain more by your new behaviour. You will not be able to control your behaviour until you are familiar with and able to control its rewards.

Our behaviour is controlled by two deeper motives: fear (preventing something) and creation (realising something). This is called 'thinking in terms of consequences'. The core of Authentic Leadership is to let the creation motive drive your behaviour and to recognise fear motives and turn them into creation motives. Authentic Leadership is being able to lead yourself and others according to the creation motive. It will help to have a clear vision of what you are striving for which will enable you to filter in the information required to realise your goal. A strong vision changes your perception of the world around you and influences your selective perception.

If a certain story is firmly established in your inner world, your behaviour will (subconsciously) lead you to it. We call this process a 'self-fulfilling prophecy'. If fears continue to drive your behaviour, they are very likely to come true in the long run as a result of a negative self-fulfilling prophecy. If a challenging vision drives your behaviour, this vision is very likely to be realised in the long run as the result of a positive self-fulfilling prophecy. Behaviour which strengthens a self-fulfilling prophecy is your self-talk. 'Self-talk' means telling yourself what you think of a particular situation. Negative self-talk brings you down, positive self-talk lifts you.

Being responsible is very worthwhile. But what are you responsible for? Although you're not always responsible for the things that happen to you, you are always responsible for the choices you make in reference to a situation. You are also responsible for the positive and negative consequences that follow from these choices, as far as they can be reasonably foreseen.

'Responsibility' should not be confused with guilt. Many people waste time on feelings of guilt. Past guilt can be turned into responsibility for the here and now.

The problem on the behavioural layer is defined as: What should I do to solve my problem with my environment? What should I do to feel happy again? You have four options: 1) complain, 2) act, 3) lower your expectations, 4) leave (use the mnemonic CALL). Whatever your choice, you will be responsible for the positive and negative consequences that follow from it.

3
The Skills Layer

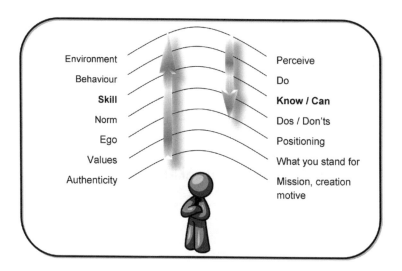

Environment	Perceive
Behaviour	Do
Skill	**Know / Can**
Norm	Dos / Don'ts
Ego	Positioning
Values	What you stand for
Authenticity	Mission, creation motive

Why is it that some people are able to deal with problems constructively while others always end up fighting? Why is it that you always know what is expected of you with some bosses while with others everything is chaotic? How can you give commitment meaning? How can you motivate yourself and others? How can you put right your mistakes? In the first two chapters I discussed the kinds of problems that can be defined on the environmental and behavioural layers. In this chapter I will deal with the skills layer and how you can deal with issues. Imagine having decided to deal with a problem in your environment. The problem will then be redefined on this layer. The question becomes *how* I should go about dealing with the problem and how I can prepare for doing so using a step-by-step plan. The most relevant communication skills are also dealt with.

In the past you will have learned many skills, both consciously and subconsciously. Numerous examples of dealing with particular situations are stored in your inner world. You use your skills to behave effectively in a certain environment or situation. You can sit, talk, catch a ball and manage a group because you have developed these skills over the years, often without being aware of it. They are usually used subconsciously, and that's the intention. You learn from experience which skills are the most effective, and eventually you start to use them automatically. Your challenge in this chapter is to try to learn a few (new) skills. The aim is to bring out your strong points, so that you can work and live together more effectively with the people around you. Skills can also be used to deceive others, to play political games or to manipulate; in doing so, you engage the fear motives of others. Although this can be very effective, it is not my mission. Moreover, I believe that this approach is only successful in the short-term, so I do not encourage it.

PROJECTING PROBLEMS ONTO THE SKILLS LAYER

The problem is redefined on the skills layer. So far the problems have been defined as:

- My environment is the problem (environmental layer).

- What should I do to solve my problem with my environment? What should I do to feel happy again? (behavioural layer).

If you choose to deal with your environment, the problem will be redefined on the skills layer as:

> *How can I influence my environment*
> *(in order to feel happy again)?*

Taking the example of the controlling boss, this means: How can I influence my boss *(in order to feel happy again)*?

If you want to learn how to influence your environment, you should first know what to expect from the outcome. When there is a problem *reality is falling short of your expectations*. Therefore, first describe what your expectations look like in an ideal world. What are you really hoping to achieve? You will find that a lot of people don't progress beyond defining a problem. If you set to work in this way, you will not make any progress. Try to formulate the desired outcomes by taking the problems you encounter along the way as your reference point. You may need some help from others here, and it may be important to ask for help from the very people you're having problems with. However, make it clear that your intention is positive. This means that it is understood that you want to work constructively towards a solution, instead of ending up finger-pointing. A positive intention means that you want to elevate your environment to a higher level.

PREPARING FOR ACTION

When problems arise between you and (an)other person(s), it is advisable to follow the step-by-step plan given below. We will take the problem of the controlling boss as an example here. 'My boss is so controlling that I have no room for manoeuvre, in the broadest sense. He gives me instructions, and if I don't follow them, we immediately get into a conflict and he starts to issue threats. He doesn't really listen to me. He always knows best. He has little confidence in me. He simply doesn't take me seriously. He sees to it that I don't develop further. He's really just securing his own future. Because of him, I don't enjoy going to work anymore.' On the behavioural layer, the problem has already been translated into 'What should you *do* to solve the problem with your boss?'.

1. What interests are at stake?

- I want to work constructively with my boss.

- I want to enjoy going to work.

- I want to take more responsibility.

- I want to achieve good results.

- I want to develop further.

- I want to receive more recognition for the work I do.

- I want more of my suggestions to be taken up.

- I want my boss to listen to me more.

2. What are the interests of your environment?

- My boss wants a well-oiled management team so that achieves results.

- He doesn't want to pay much attention to his team.

- He wants to feel happy at work.

- He wants to control the process.

- He wants to be respected by his team.

- He wants to receive recognition for the work he does.

- He wants to be listened to.

- He wants to further his career.

- He doesn't want to encounter much resistance from the departments.

3. What interests do you share?

- Realising a good collaboration.

- Achieving good results.

- Receiving recognition from management.

- Receiving recognition from colleagues.

- Being able to improve yourself.

- Feeling happy at work.

4. Which interests conflict?

• Being free versus being controlled.

• Demanding attention versus paying attention.

5. Describe as clearly as possible your image of a desired future (taking account of the preceding points).

A collaboration in which we respect each other, share the right information, support each other to achieve the best results and receive recognition for this (you can probably assume that this is also what your boss wants).

6. Request a meeting in which you and your boss will make proper agreements about your differences.

This concerns the issues of freedom versus control and demanding attention versus paying attention.

7. Just do it!

Although there are numerous reasons not to enter into this discussion, try to give it a chance of succeeding (a suggestion is to use feedforward as a skill in this example).

TRY THIS...

Try to take the preparatory steps set out in the step-by-step plan for one of your problems.

RELEVANT SKILLS

Which relevant skills can help you advance further towards Authentic Leadership? The following skills will be dealt with:

• Gaining insight into the management cycle;

• being able to apply the SHAPE process;

• using feedforward;

- being able to give compliments.

Other skills and insights that may benefit you are featured on the website. Examine the parts which you think could be useful:

- Reprimanding;

- communicating a decision;

- offering apologies;

- negotiating;

- coaching;

- peer group coaching.

The skills that are explained below and on the website are intended to build bridges between you and the person you're speaking to. The skills have unique applications in specific situations. You can master a skill by repeatedly putting it into practice.

Gaining insight into the management cycle

A process always starts with the intention of doing things more effectively, solving problems, starting something new, heading in a (new) direction (e.g. increasing your market share, increasing customer satisfaction, solving staff problems, normalising the relationship with your neighbours).

The second step in the cycle (see Figure 3.1) is to put the intention into concrete terms by making it measurable and, therefore, verifiable. The intention becomes an objective (e.g. increasing market share by 13 per cent; increasing customer satisfaction from 6.5 to 7.5; increasing employee satisfaction from 5 to 7; the neighbours keeping the noise down after 10 p.m.). An intention can be worked out into several (sub)objectives. By translating an intention into an objective and then communicating this objective, you will manage the expectations of all the parties involved and will be able to check whether all the parties are striving for the same results. The objectives that are set should be Specific, Measurable, Acceptable, Realistic and Time-bound (SMART).

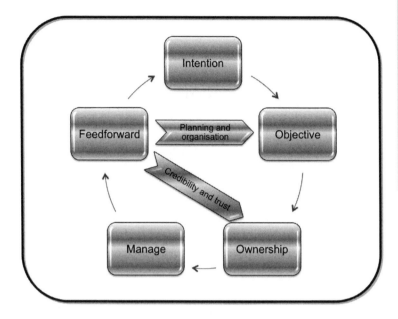

Figure 3.1 The management cycle

A step that is often skipped, particularly in the business world, is that of checking ownership. Do the parties involved really want to *own* the objectives? Are they prepared to accept the consequences? Commitment means at least three things: (1) really going for something, (2) wanting to be held accountable for it and (3) holding others accountable. Ownership does not necessarily mean that you think there are no better objectives. You may have a different personal preference; this should be brought up when the objective is set. When, at some point, a decision is made, the question will be whether you will faithfully agree to the decision, *own* the decision. A common management dilemma is whether you should be able to express your doubts (if any) about the quality of the objective to others. Going by my experience, I would advise against this. You jointly decide on the arguments for selecting an objective, and you use these arguments to communicate the objective to others. Then you let it be known that, following in-depth discussions, you have committed yourself to the objective. If you are not able to commit yourself, you can choose to leave. Complaining is not an option, since that would only create uncertainty among the parties involved.

64

AUTHENTIC LEADERSHIP

After ownership has been assigned, the realisation process is monitored and controlled. This is referred to as 'managing towards results'. Feedforward follows on as a result of these monitoring activities: you give feedforward so that you will be able to do things even more effectively in the future. If things are going well and the objective is achieved, this is followed by a compliment and by studying how the things that went well can be replicated in subsequent management cycles. If things are not going well, look to see what lessons can be learned.

Feedforward gives you several options. If an objective is not achieved, its level of difficulty is often considered when feedforward is given (it was too ambitious, there wasn't enough time, something else cropped up, the market wasn't favourable, etc.). Giving feedforward about an objective concerns the planning and organisation of working methods, but it is much more interesting to give feedforward about ownership: if you, as a manager, educator or teacher, learn at the very last minute that an objective will not be achieved, you will have another problem on your hands: someone has said 'yes' but done 'no'. To what extent will you be able to trust the next 'yes'? In this way, you give feedforward about someone's credibility. An effective norm you can agree upon is to inform the interested parties well before the deadline that an objective will not be achieved. This then applies to all agreements you make in order to protect everyone's credibility. On the basis of the results of feedforward, the management cycle starts again.

TRY THIS...

Look for three objectives in your environment that have yet to be achieved and determine the management cycle stage at which improvements could be made.

Look at how you worked out your step-by-step plan from the last exercise and see if you would like to rephrase your answers as a result of the management cycle.

Applying the SHAPE technique (sharing perceptions)

As we have seen, it is very difficult to speak in terms of 'truths' when you realise that selective perception distorts our truths. It is very important to realise this if you want to be able to communicate properly with others. SHAPE stands for '*sharing perceptions*'. Its six steps form the basic ingredients for dialogues, negotiations, coaching interviews, feedforward and dealing with resistance. The SHAPE process takes account of selective perception. SHAPE can be used as a technique, but the process actually goes much further. SHAPE is based on the belief that two truths can – and may – exist side by side, even if another person's truth is diametrically opposed to yours. There are always several possibilities.

Everyone has the tendency to go on the defensive or offensive, especially when attacked (*fight or flight*). In communication, the winner is the one who is the loudest in expressing her opinion. And the objective is that someone wins. The purpose of the SHAPE process is not that someone wins, but that the best solution is found. It is important that you master this technique so that you will be in control of the communication process.

Step 1 Focus attention on the other person's perception (keep asking questions and listen actively) Try to fully understand the other person before giving your opinion. If there are no time constraints, you don't have to worry about the other person having too much speaking time; your turn will come. Keep asking questions until you understand the other person. You are actually giving the other person the opportunity to put his cards on the table. What are his views? What are his interests? What does it mean to him? Keep asking questions until you fully understand the other person's perception. You will then know the other person's image (as well as your own), and the other person will appreciate having been able to finish what he had to say.

Step 2 'Message understood' (let the other person know that you have understood his perception) If you understand the other person's perception, inform him of this. Acknowledge you have understood his message: your image is clear, thanks. This makes for a calm communication process. The other person does not have to put forward any new arguments; you no longer have to be convinced. An acknowledgement can pertain to the content or the emotional charge of a message. So, on the one hand, you can briefly summarise the other person's image ('So you mean ...') or appraise it ('I'm glad you said that') and, on the other, you can discuss your feelings ('I sense that you're disappointed'). An acknowledgement is intended to leave the other person's image intact. What you often (unfortunately) hear is 'Yes, but ...' Delete this response from your system. A 'yes, but' response is really a spontaneous lead-in to an objection, that is, it simply means 'no'. Met with a 'yes, but', the other person will counter with his own 'yes, but' response. This is counterproductive. Try to leave the person's image intact in the acknowledgement stage. Don't attack the image, even if you don't agree with it.

Step 3 Explain my perception (this is what I think) You can sometimes skip steps 3 and 4 and continue with step 5. However, if you have a completely different perception, it is advisable to place your perception *alongside* the other person's perception (instead of replacing it with yours). If necessary, start by saying 'I understand your perception. Do you mind if I place our opinions side-by-side?' A rhetorical question which will of course be answered affirmatively.

Step 4 Ask the receiver to acknowledge he has understood your perception Before starting the discussion, ask if the other person has fully understood your perception without expecting him to agree with it. You have done your best to understand the other person, so you may now expect him to do his best to understand you. Steps 1–4 can be repeated several times, until both images are completely clear for both parties.

Step 5 Finding the best solution Two perceptions are now on the table. It is important now to find the best solution based on these two perceptions by continuing to ask questions, looking into alternatives, etc. Future-oriented questions that are useful here include 'How can we ... ?', 'How can I...?', 'How do you feel about ...?', 'How shall we proceed from here?' Try to understand each other every step of the way.

Step 6 Make concrete agreements Wrap things up with a concrete solution and an action that can be carried out.

TRY THIS…

In the months ahead, make a conscious effort to apply the SHAPE process during discussions or when you encounter resistance. You stand to gain from this immediately, although you will have to get used to holding back your opinion.

Using feedforward

Feedforward is a skill you will need if you want to persuade someone to change her behaviour. You will discover that it is vital when you want to make changes in your environment. Although feedforward resembles feedback, feedback is characterised by talking about the past, while feedforward is future-oriented. Many people are slightly afraid to hold others accountable for their behaviour. This is understandable, since it involves a certain risk. In general, people are afraid that holding others accountable will harm their relationship. This is a realistic risk if you have the wrong intentions. If you just want to punish a person, she will hold this against you, but if you want to use feedforward to elevate others or your collaboration to a higher level, you will not run this risk. However, it is important to express your positive intention very explicitly.

Step 1 Emphasise your positive intention Your positive intention is usually focused on the other person's further development or on improving your relationship, and is always future-oriented.

Step 2 Describe the behaviour you see It is important that you take account of your selective perception here. Tell the other person what behaviour you have observed. Do this matter-of-factly. Don't make any accusations, and leave out value judgements for the time being. 'I've noted that our appointments have been cancelled four times' has a different ring to it than, 'You don't think my input is important.' The latter immediately makes a value judgement, and it remains to be seen if it is actually correct. Therefore, try to stay as close to the truth as possible in this step.

Step 3 Describe the associations or feelings this causes This is where you indicate explicitly how you regard the situation. Tell the other person how you see it. Tell the other person how this affects you. Leave it at that; this is also the truth, since the things you think and feel are your truth. By following steps 2 and 3 in that order, you will give the other person enough room to avoid directly going on the defensive or counter-offensive. For example, 'That strikes me as if you don't think my input is important' or 'This makes me feel undervalued' describes how it affects you, irrespective of whether this was the other person's intention.

Step 4 Check if your image has been understood You will see a link with the SHAPE process here. Before entering into a discussion, ask if the other person understands your perception. 'Can you understand that this is how I feel about it?' You can usually count on the other person understanding your image if you have properly carried out steps 2 and 3. If that is the case, you can continue with step 7. If your image is not understood at this point, continue with steps 5 and 6.

Step 5 (in case your perception has not been understood) Ask the other person her perception 'How do you see things?'

Step 6 'Message understood' 'I understand what you mean.' Steps 2–6 can be repeated several times.

Step 7 Find a solution 'How shall we proceed from here?' 'What can we agree about this?'

Step 8 Make a concrete agreement 'We agree that …'

If the mood deteriorates during a conversation, reiterate your positive intention. You really want to elevate your relationship, or the person, to a higher level. It is advisable to prepare steps 1–3 properly. Also start thinking about possible solutions. If you really mean well, the other person will eventually recognise this. When you gain more experience in this, you will even see that it's rewarding to help the people around you to develop further. It is of course also important that you receive proper feedforward here. Even if the other person's intentions towards you are not at all positive, you will be able to change the course of the conversation in that direction. In fact as receiver, you follow the same steps.

TRY THIS...

If you want to confront someone in the weeks ahead, prepare for
the meeting using the step-by-step plan set out above.

Being able to pay compliments

Feedforward also means that you want to reward and reinforce good behaviour. Giving a compliment is an important skill to that end. Receiving
recognition is one of the prime motivators. By paying a compliment, you
allow a certain self-image of a person to take up an important place in
her inner world. As a result, the person develops further, sees more opportunities and gains more self-confidence. This is not only true of young
persons, but also of experienced board members. However, the problem
is that we often find it difficult to accept compliments (I will discuss the
reason for this in detail in Chapter 7). For the time being, it is important
to realise that the manner in which you pay a compliment determines
whether or not the compliment will be allowed through the other person's filters. Four simple but relevant suggestions are given below.

Compliments should always be sincere: people intuitively know if a compliment is only being made for the effect, that is, that you are only making
it for your own benefit.

Compliments should be concrete: the more concrete a compliment, the
greater the likelihood that it will be allowed through the other person's
filters. 'That's a good report' is less likely to register than 'It's a good
report, largely because of the thorough way you came to your recom-
mendations.' Try, as much as possible, to see the world through the other
person's eyes here.

Compliments don't have to be spontaneous: some people think that you can
only pay a compliment if it is spontaneous and directly follows an action.
Although this might be better, it is definitely not necessary. As long as the
other person's compliment is sincere, wouldn't you appreciate a compliment about an activity that was completed some time ago?

Don't be afraid to pay compliments: compliments are usually not expressed because 'people don't expect to hear them'. But don't be mistaken, there are a huge number of reasons to pay compliments. Although people may not receive compliments very well, several investigations have shown that it is the key source of motivation. Just do it! If the other person reacts strangely, that is largely his problem. Also realise that there is a causal relationship between the number of compliments you pay and the number of compliments you receive. When you open your filters wider to compliments, you will see that you will receive more compliments.

TRY THIS...

Think back to yesterday, and the situations in which you paid or could have paid a compliment. Check whether the compliments you paid were sufficiently sincere and concrete. And check if there is an opportunity to pay a compliment in the near future. Just do it!

SUMMARY

Having identified a problem on the environmental layer, you may have decided to deal with your environment on the behavioural layer. The problem on the skills layer is defined as 'How should I influence my environment (to feel happy again)?'

If you want to deal with the problems that exist between you and others, it is advisable to follow the step-by-step plan:

1. What interests are at stake?

2. Get to know what the interests of your environment are.

3. What interests do you have in common?

4. Which interests conflict?

5. Describe as clearly as possible your image of a desired future (taking account of the preceding points).

6. Prepare a meeting in which you will make proper agreements about your differences.

7. Just do it!

The trick is to present things with a positive intention in mind. A positive intention means that you want to elevate your environment or your relationship to a higher level. You will need this insight for the authenticity layer.

The following four skills were discussed (other skills are featured on the website (www.authentiekleiderschap.nl/en):

1. The management cycle, consisting of logical steps that may help identify problems more effectively.

2. The SHAPE technique, a method of communication in which your perception and that of another person can exist side-by-side, enabling you to carry on a dialogue on equal terms.

3. Feedforward, a direct way of holding others to account, in which 'truth' and feelings have been separated and a positive intention is the guiding force.

4. Paying compliments; there is a causal relationship between the number of compliments you pay and the number of compliments you receive.

4
The norms layer

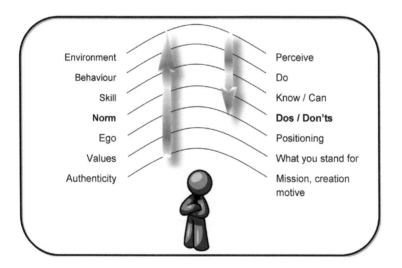

Environment	Perceive
Behaviour	Do
Skill	Know / Can
Norm	**Dos / Don'ts**
Ego	Positioning
Values	What you stand for
Authenticity	Mission, creation motive

An important aspect of management courses is giving participants the skills to give co-workers, colleagues and managers feedforward. Trainers hope that by understanding this communication model and regularly practicing it course members will gain confidence in using it. It often becomes apparent that course members are quite capable of using feedforward, but rarely do so. The trainer asks, 'You know how to give feedforward, don't you?' At which point the course members point out that in practice things work differently. These management, sales and communication courses are ignoring the norms that are an important phenomenon working in the minds of people when they make decisions about which skills to use.

This chapter addresses the following questions: What are norms? To what extent do they influence your behaviour? Where do our norms come from? I will distinguish between restrictive and stimulating norms. You will also learn that you not only have a comfort zone, but also a growth zone, a recklessness zone and a contraction zone.

WHERE DO OUR NORMS COME FROM?

The term 'norm' is derived from the word 'normalise'. *A norm is a specific rule of conduct, judgement, standard or assessment.* The norms layer is important since most interpersonal conflicts arise here (because we don't all follow the same norms).

What is special about the norms layer is that people are continually labelling, without being aware of it. From the moment you picked up this book, you started appraising it. 'Is it any good?' 'Have I ever heard of it?' 'Who's the author?' 'Is it a thick book?' When you think back to the process in your inner world, you will see that labelling is wired into our systems. After all, you ask yourself the following when you make an assessment: How should I label this information? What are the potential consequences? What are the potential courses of action? What produces the greatest rewards? The norm you adhere to in a certain situation determines your behaviour in your environment.

As a child, you quickly learned about norms when you were made aware of what you could and could not do. This was sometimes made clear to you when you hurt yourself. At other times this was made clear to you by the people around you. You learned how to behave: not to eat with your mouth open, not to tease your sister, not to steal, not to make too much noise, etc. In other words, you were often told what was not allowed. Incidentally, educators are in reasonable agreement that it is more effective to tell a child what it should do (or what norms it should comply with): keep your mouth shut when you eat, be nice to your sister, leave that alone, calm down, etc. Your community also taught you norms. What kind of behaviour is tolerated and what is not? You simply complied with these norms to avoid getting into too much trouble or just to receive recognition. You often didn't think about it; that's simply the way things were.

This could sometimes prove to be difficult at a later stage, as the process by which we acquire norms can make their real sense somewhat obscure. For example, when you have an itch behind your ears, you scratch a little. That makes sense. But when you have an itch in other parts of your body, you'll think twice about scratching yourself in public. Why? Because that's not proper!

You also picked up norms in school and at university, from friends and lecturers. And it quickly became clear to you that all environments set their own norms. When you were with friends, you observed different norms from those you observed with your parents-in-law. You observe different norms when you are alone or with others.

At an even later stage, you were faced with an altogether different set of norms at work. What is and is not allowed here? Should I adopt a directive management style or are they really expecting a participative style? In every new job, you learned that you had to adapt yourself to the applicable norms.

Because everyone (and that includes you) has a need to be accepted in one way or another, everyone complies with these rules. Just think of 'recognition', one of the most important rewards discussed in Chapter 2. Because people have a strong need to be included, you quickly learn to adapt to the norms that apply in or are dictated by your environment. You are then driven by *external norms*. If you want to feel at home in different environments, this means that you will have to observe different external norms. That shouldn't be a problem. However, it becomes a problem when you see that norms are imposed which you do not wish to accept. Incidentally, not all norms are equally important. You sometimes accept an external norm, even though it is not your norm. For example, if you're asked to observe a moment of silence before a meal, you won't give it a second's thought, even if you're not used to doing this at home. However, if you're asked to discriminate against someone on the grounds of colour, you will (I hope) refuse to do so.

You become wiser over the years and you feel less pressure to comply with external norms. You have been through so much, or have given so much thought to things, that you don't simply want to please your environment by complying with its norms. Because some norms are firmly established in your inner world, you start to live – following an internal assessment – more according to these (internal) norms. *Internal norms* are rules of conduct you have chosen for yourself because you are who you are. They follow from your values and mission (see Chapters 6 and 7). Internal norms are closer to your heart than external norms. So when you are driven by internal norms, your position in your environment is more independent.

RESTRICTIVE AND STIMULATING NORMS ON THE COMFORT ZONE

Restrictive and stimulating norms

You will sometimes realise that you know how to deal with a problem, but that something is holding you back. It doesn't feel right. You can distinguish between restrictive and stimulating norms here. *Stimulating norms* are those that encourage you to display desired behaviour. They are creation-driven. They come from your desires. *Restrictive norms* hold you back and are fear-driven. They help you to avoid a negative consequence. Sometimes it is difficult to recognise why you don't behave in a certain way, even though you know it would be good for you. You know what to do, how to do it and yet, you don't do it. A restrictive norm is often at play here.

Comfort zone and growth zone

It would be interesting to examine the effect of restrictive and stimulating norms on your comfort zone. A comfort zone is a subjectively perceived environment that feels safe and comfortable. These zones differ from person to person. Some people feel perfectly at ease when they give a presentation in front of a room full of people, while others feel that this falls outside their comfort zone. It is not only individuals who have a comfort zone; teams and organisations also have one. Humans have a natural tendency to seek the outer limits of their comfort zone. We are creative and inquisitive beings. The will to develop is simply in our DNA. And you develop by stepping outside of your comfort zone. We have already seen that a creation motive tempts us and makes us long for more. You get a wonderful feeling every time you realise a new creation. When you have achieved something, you may, after a while, try to expand your comfort zone further in search of new and sometimes more challenging situations. People develop most just outside their comfort zone. The responsible stimulating norm can be expressed as follows: *'I'd like to step outside of my comfort zone, because ... (fill in the creation).'*

However, there are also norms that protect you, that ensure that you don't take irresponsible risks. These are controlled by the fear motive. We call these norms 'restrictive norms'. The sentence that goes with them is *'You'd better not leave your comfort zone, because ... (fill in the fear).'*

This is the self-talk you came across in Chapter 2. Both norms are useful. Both of them lead to a reward. The stimulating norm allows you to enjoy a creation, the restrictive norm stops you in your tracks to save you from a bad ending. So you can see that there is a clash, as it were, happening at the edge of your comfort zone: a clash between your restrictive and stimulating norms. You can recognise this by carefully listening to your self-talk, which is telling you why you should or should not do something. There are two different voices, whispering different norms in your head. Unfortunately, when you approach the edge of your comfort zone, you will hear only one voice, that of your restrictive norm. This is because we perceive fear quicker than creation. As you approach the edge of your comfort zone, your fear-driven voice speaks, drowning out your loving, creation-driven voice. It is therefore important for your further development to be aware of both norms and also to consider the stimulating norm so that you can carefully weigh up whether you should step outside of your comfort zone or not (see also Figure 4.1).

You can follow some simple steps if you feel that something is holding you back.

1. Write the restrictive norm (self-talk) down:

Restrictive norm: You'd better not (behaviour), otherwise … (fear).

Example:

Restrictive norm: You'd better not (confront), otherwise (it will harm your relationship).

2. Now try to describe the stimulating norm:

Stimulating norm: You'd better (behaviour), because this … (creation).

Example:

Stimulating norm: You'd better (confront), because this (could improve your relationship).

3. Make a conscious choice! Now that you have described the stimulating norm, you can make a more informed decision. Think of the following proposition here: whether you are prepared to change your behaviour (step out of your comfort zone) will depend on the benefits or rewards of an alternative behaviour (stimulating norms).

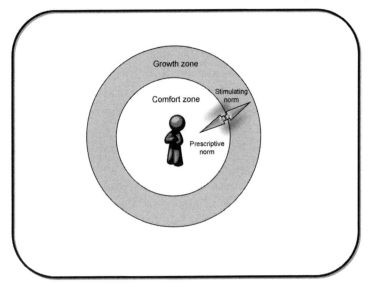

Figure 4.1 Comfort and growth zones with restrictive and stimulating norms

In Appendix 1 I have translated a few common restrictive norms into stimulating norms.

The restrictive norm can be overruled by largely focusing on the reward of the stimulating norm. Replace your negative self-talk with positive self-talk; don't stay in your comfort zone by force of habit. That would be a shame, since your *growth zone* lies just outside your comfort zone. You will enter a new environment. You will learn, develop, grow, create. When you step out of your comfort zone and achieve results, this will give you a real thrill and an enormous sense of pride. You are extremely focused in your growth zone and you really have to use your skills. We can talk about this zone as an area where you can achieve a state of *flow*. It seems as if you use the rewards of your fear and creation motives here: you enjoy your creation and you are also careful not to let things go wrong. An authentic leader continually seeks out this *growth zone*, because she wants the creation motive to lead the way as much as possible in exciting situations, both for herself and for the people she manages. Being successful in the growth zone gives a sense of personal fulfilment that we want to share with others.

It is perfectly okay to stay in your comfort zone after you have weighed up the restrictive and stimulating norms, because then you will have considered the pros and cons and accepted the consequences. You should also realise that stepping out of your comfort zone always involves some stress. It is not called a comfort zone for nothing! You don't know for sure whether things will work out so there is always an element of uncertainty. Authentic leaders who do this often develop, from experience, a higher level of self-confidence. They get used to the uncertainty and are more likely to take risks and let their stimulating norms lead the way. They can go into an unknown environment with the greatest degree of self-confidence.

Reckless zone

Developing yourself and others is fantastic and builds self-confidence. However, make sure that you, and others, don't venture too far from the comfort zone all at once, as beyond it lies the 'reckless' or 'panic zone' (see Figure 4.2). This is where your worst fears may come true: you may be rejected, lose your position, suffer physical injury. You want to get out quickly. The reckless zone can either be reality or your own perception; you think that you are being harmed and get in a panic about it and, as a result, actually be harmed.

If you spend too much time in this zone, your original comfort zone may even shrink. Your self-confidence will diminish. You will become risk-averse ('That won't happen to me again!'). For example, if you have only just started to learn to give presentations and you are put in front of a large, critical audience, your panic reaction may result in you never giving a presentation again, not even in front of a small group.

Contraction zone

People who panic sometimes make their comfort zone so small that they end up in the *contraction zone*. They're on automatic pilot when they do things. Their behaviour is no longer driven by a creation motive. If you stay in this zone for a long time, you will become incredibly bored and less and less happy with yourself. You will feel that you are capable of more, but won't do anything about it. This gives you a frustrated, rotten feeling. You see this in employees who have become set in their ways. They no longer want to undertake anything new, although they are not really satisfied with the way things are. When you look into this, you will often find that these employees left their comfort zone with the best of intentions at one time or another, but then fell flat on their face. Incidentally, this may have happened years ago. They have therefore become disenchanted and may have made their comfort zones a little too small. Although they are capable of doing more than they are currently doing, they are afraid to, or have lost the will to. It is extremely rewarding to rebuild the self-confidence of this group of people as their 'old' creation motive is still lurking somewhere deep inside them. It is dangerous to stay too long in the contraction zone, as you run the risk of creating a negative self-fulfilling prophecy when you let your restrictive norms lead the way for too long and as a consequence your fears become reality. We came across this phenomenon when discussing the rewards of fear motives.

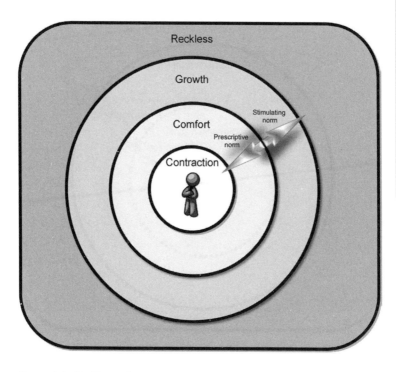

Figure 4.2 Reckless and contraction zones

Another minor warning: restrictive norms don't just go away. Restrictive norms can be sought out, put on the table and discussed, as in the step-by-step plan set out above. You can put stimulating norms alongside them and let them lead the way so that you end up in the growth zone. However, as you develop further, your comfort zone will expand to form a 'new' outer limit (Figure 4.3). What is fascinating is that the same restrictive and stimulating norms will battle it out again. This means that, once you have described them properly for yourself, your team or your organisation, you will be able to predict future clashes and act accordingly. If you experience a similar clash at a later stage, your reaction need not be one of frustration ('I haven't learned anything from it!'). No, you have learned a lot, your comfort zone has expanded, you have developed and your restrictive norm will try to 'save' you again at a newly-formed outer limit. And now you know that the same stimulating norm may tempt you again.

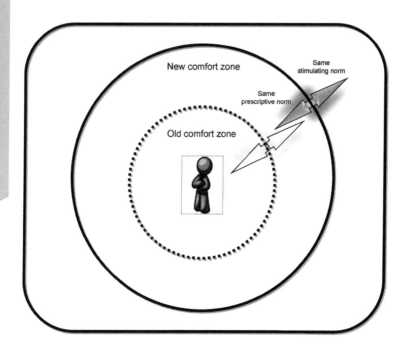

Figure 4.3 The same norms at the outer limit of the comfort zone

You might now begin to realise that the norms layer is the most important layer on which we decide how we behave. For your own behavioural
development, and that of your team or organisation, it is therefore one
of the most important layers to examine in greater detail. In Chapter 6
you will learn how to use the above insights to sustain a cultural development programme, or to ensure that people embrace new behaviour.

We have brought together all the behavioural rewards on the comfort
zone in Figure 4.4. You are enticed out of your comfort zone by a stimulating norm that represents your longing for a desired creation. Although
it is great to step out of your comfort zone, be careful not to get carried
away by taking excessive risks and ending up in the recklessness zone.
You are kept within your comfort zone by a restrictive norm that represents the avoidance of a negative consequence. It is fine to stay in your
comfort zone, but be careful not to get too settled there as staying in
your contraction zone for too long could create a negative self-fulfilling
prophecy.

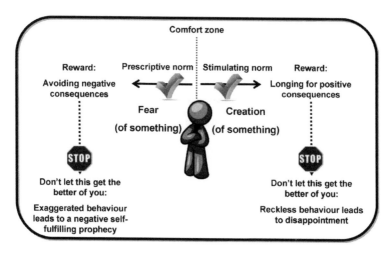

Figure 4.4 Rewards at the outer limit of the comfort zone

PROJECTING PROBLEMS ONTO THE NORMS LAYER

By making a distinction between restrictive and stimulating norms, you redefine the problem in a specific way. So far the problems have been defined as:

- My environment is the problem (environmental layer).

- What should I do to solve my problem with my environment? What should I do to feel happy again? (behavioural layer).

- How should I influence my environment (in order to feel happy again)? (skills layer).

The problem on the norms layer can be defined as follows:

Which stimulating or restrictive norm should take precedence in order for me to solve my problem with my environment?

Taking the example of the controlling boss, the problem can be defined as 'How can I let my stimulating norm take precedence over my restrictive norm so that I can solve my problem with my boss?' As you saw in the step-by-step plan, it is advisable in such situations to describe what restrictive and stimulating norms you observe in respect of your proposed decision to do something about your environment. Simply writing down both norms will often enable you to decide on a mode of behaviour. An example of the stimulating and restrictive norms in respect of your intended meeting with your boss is given in Table 4.1.

Table 4.1 Examples of stimulating and restrictive norms

Restrictive norms	Stimulating norms
I'd better not confront him, because…	I'd better confront him, because…
If it doesn't work out, this will harm the relationship and may damage my image.	It's good for my self-esteem.
People will think I'm a busybody, since it's his responsibility, and not mine, to create a good atmosphere in the unit.	This will enable him to develop further.
	I can improve the relationship.
	It's good to be less dependent on others.
	I will have more influence.
	I will be more likely to feel happy again.
	The atmosphere will improve.
	It will take less energy out of me.
	It will take less energy out of others.

What is difficult about your restrictive and stimulating norms is that both of them feel like the truth to you. However, your selective perception also plays a role here. It may help you to call into question the rewards of the restrictive norm so that you can make them smaller. In doing so, you will examine your own norms in greater detail, enabling you to make a conscious choice. Are you going to stay in your comfort zone and listen to your restrictive norms, or are you going to opt for growth and let your stimulating norms lead the way? Two examples:

1. *My boss is responsible for creating a pleasant atmosphere in the department, not me.* Yes, it's part of his job, but no, that isn't an excuse to do nothing. If you're unhappy, you can take responsibility for doing something about it yourself, even if the other person doesn't take his responsibility.

2. *You're not supposed to correct your boss.* You're not correcting him; you're giving him advice to enable him to become more successful. Everyone wants good advice from others, so that they can become more effective or happier. However, make sure that you explicitly prepare and express these positive intentions.

Don't underestimate how difficult it is to seek out your restrictive norms. You're often not aware of your hidden fears. This is why it is all the more important to examine them. There may be other reasons why you're afraid to behave in a certain way. These often have to do with the egos that are getting in your way (see Chapter 5). A good way to solve a problem on the norms layer is to ask yourself which values or mission you would like to guide you in your behaviour. I will discuss this in Chapters 6 and 7.

SUMMARY

Your behaviour is driven by norms. A norm is a specific rule of conduct, judgement, standard or assessment. You are continually (subconsciously) labelling your environment. Every environment has its own set of norms or rules of conduct. Norms which are dictated by your environment are called 'external norms'. Because you spend time in different environments, you may observe different external norms.

You can also be driven by your internal norms. Internal norms are norms that stem from your values. If you grew up in a certain environment, many external norms will have been internalised.

Stimulating norms are those that encourage you to display desired behaviour and are creation-driven. Restrictive norms hold you back and are fear-driven. Your restrictive and stimulating norms clash at the outer limit of your comfort zone. Your growth zone lies just outside your comfort zone. An authentic leader seeks out this zone, since this is where you can develop to the optimum and feel happy as a result. The recklessness zone lies too far from the comfort zone. This is where you may be rejected, lose your position or suffer physical injury. You don't want to go there. If you have often experienced disappointment, your comfort zone may shrink to a contraction zone. In this zone, you perform below your potential and fall prey to boredom.

The problem on the norms layer can be defined as 'Which stimulating or restrictive norm should take precedence in order for me to solve the problem with my environment?'

Because you are not usually very conscious of your restrictive norms, it is advisable to make an overview of both your restrictive and stimulating norms. You can use this overview to decide how to deal with a restrictive norm.

5
The ego layer

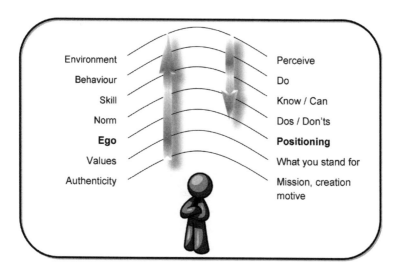

Environment	Perceive
Behaviour	Do
Skill	Know / Can
Norm	Dos / Don'ts
Ego	**Positioning**
Values	What you stand for
Authenticity	Mission, creation motive

You have reached the core of the book. The ego layer lies between the norms and values layers and is the deepest layer on which an environment can exert influence. On this layer you will find the various egos you can call into play to influence others. Although egos are useful mechanisms, you must be careful not to let them get the better of you for too long, otherwise you may fall prey to the very things you're trying to avoid. In this chapter I discuss what egos are and how they work. You will find out why you call them into play, what the corresponding risks and benefits are and how you can deal with them when you see that they don't produce the desired results. I will discuss this at length, since calling your exaggerated egos into play is one of the main and least recognisable barriers that can obstruct your further development; you could call this a 'glass ceiling'. This is because egos (subconsciously) develop over the years. You are not aware that patterns and sub-personalities have built up in your system, which are holding back something of your authenticity. I will look at eight relevant egos and describe how they are called into play, where and how they benefit (or harm) you and when it is better to overrule them. This is more often the case than you might think, since egos often prevent you from experiencing a sense of fulfilment.

You will find that some insights may feel quite confrontational, as it is unpleasant to learn that your behaviour is often controlled by your ego. It is also not nice to learn that you often (subconsciously) try to force your position in a group. Comfort yourself with the thought that you are not the only one. Just look around you. Everyone you meet has the same insecurities, only they do not yet have the capacity to deal with them. You can free yourself from the egos that hinder you and let your authenticity lead the way. The choice is yours.

WHAT IS AN EGO?

In this book 'ego' is defined as a *self-image that has previously helped you to position yourself in a certain way in relation to your environment*. People have several egos they might fall back on. A good example of an ego is 'the Nice One'. The Nice One wants to be liked by the people around him. He tries to achieve this by being nice to others. He is quite capable of showing appreciation and making compliments. However, it remains to be seen if the Nice One really likes you; he may actually not like you at all. The main thing is that you like him. It is notable that this ego tries to avoid confrontations. The Nice One is also unlikely to say 'no' to people, because the result may be that they stop liking him. Why does the Nice One do these things? What is the reward? There are two possible reasons to behave in this way.

Firstly, perhaps the Nice One actually is nice and sincerely wants to compliment others in order to help them to develop further. The driving force behind his behaviour is creation. The ego is then in its prime and forms an extension of your authenticity:

- You move from the centre outwards.

- You are somebody.

- You want to create something in your environment.

- The creation motive therefore takes over.

- You stand for something (value).

- The fact that this is recognised by your environment is an added benefit, although it is not necessary. Therefore, your ego is not driving your behaviour.

- You only call your egos into play for strategic reasons, since you know that it can benefit you to create something (see also Chapters 7 and 8).

Secondly, and conversely, perhaps the Nice One wants to avoid being disliked since he holds an important (restrictive) norm: 'If the others don't like me, I'll be thrown out of the group. I will no longer make a difference.' He therefore has to be nice. The driving force behind his behaviour is fear. The reward is 'to continue to make a difference', and the Nice One achieves this by securing the recognition he receives from the people around him. The ego is then a reaction to his environment:

- You move from the outside inwards.

- You want to prevent your environment from undermining your position.

- You have to behave in a way that stops this happening.

- You do so (usually subconsciously) by calling your ego into play.

- The fear motive therefore takes over.

- You want to 'be labelled', whether the label fits or not. It is vital that you position yourself in this way.

- Your ego takes over.

An ego can come into play as an *extension of a creation* or to prevent *loss of position*. This chapter largely deals with the latter, since the greatest barriers to growth result from this.

TRY THIS …

Before we deal with the theory, try to recognise your own egos. Go to www.authentiekleiderschap.nl/en/freeegoscan. There you will find a free download for the Ego Scan light version. There is also a full version of the Ego Scan©, which will bring the exaggerated variants of your egos and your allergies to light. The free version is your first introduction to your egos. Please note: everyone has egos. In fact, all the egos discussed in this chapter are represented in your inner world. This little scan is only meant to give you a rough idea of the egos you use the most.

THE OBJECTIVE OF AN EGO

We have already seen that it makes you happy when you receive proof that you make a difference. An ego aims to position itself in a certain way in relation to others, *thereby obtaining proof it is meaningful*. You secure your position in a group by positioning yourself. This is what an ego intends to do: to be allowed to stay in the group, to ensure that you (still) make a difference and that you may still play a certain role in the group. Incidentally, although this intention is not expressed, it does (subconsciously) drive your behaviour. Therefore, your ego wants to secure your position in the group or, negatively put, prevent you from not making a difference and being thrown out of the group.

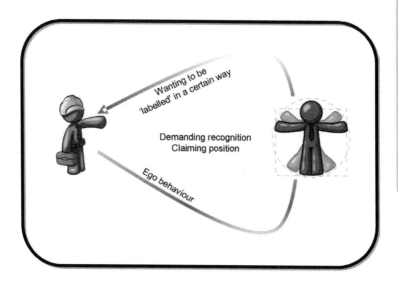

Figure 5.1 'Obtaining' proof that you make a difference

Calling an ego into play is a way to secure *recognition* (see Figure 5.1). You *demand*, as it were, recognition. You feel better when you gain it. To claim a position, an ego sees to it that 'it is labelled in a certain way'. You saw that the Nice One wants to be liked in order to be allowed to stay in the group. It looks as if your behaviour is directed at others, but your intentions tell us otherwise. In fact, your behaviour is directed at yourself.

You should note that this does not concern 'your deepest self'. It is not authentic. It's really a trick, a clever trick that you pull, usually subconsciously. You simply put on a mask. And, if you pull the trick off, it won't be for the last time. You will go on to use it so often that you are actually no longer aware that you are calling your ego into play. The mask has become more visible than your true, authentic self.

HOW ARE EGOS FORMED?

Egos are formed early in life. When you were young, you became aware that you could influence relationships. You didn't like it when you didn't get your own way. You reacted to this, and the reaction sometimes worked in your favour. For example, think back to when you were a child, and the feeling of disappointment you got when your parents didn't give you a particular toy that you wanted. If you responded to the disappointment by being very nice about it to your parents, and your 'good' behaviour was then rewarded with the desired toy an important story was created in your mind: 'If I'm nice to others, I'll get my own way.' If this trick has the same (desired) results in other situations, an ego will automatically be formed. In this case, it's the Nice One. But perhaps you responded to the disappointment by getting into a rage and screaming hysterically, and your parents gave you the toy to stop the tantrum. In this case a different ego will be formed. The fact that a child develops egos is a good thing. Egos help the child to learn that she can show her vulnerability in a group, that she can withstand group pressure, that she is not a plaything of the other group members. Egos are, in fact, properly functioning survival strategies. Egos are formed, and develop, without you being aware of it. An ego is usually formed when things in your environment are not going the way you want. You learn that a certain kind of behaviour gets you what you want so you store it as a successful trick in your behavioural repertoire.

The moment an ego is called into play can be partially inferred from the above. You often call an ego into play when you want to avoid not getting your own way, or when your position in the group has been compromised. The fear motive leads the way. You want to avoid a certain negative consequence. The environment is in fact unsafe. However, some nuance is called for here. In much the same way that 'fear' does not imply horror, 'unsafe' does not imply that your life is in danger. 'Unsafe' means that you think you will not get your own way because of something that has happened in your environment. Unsafe means that you are not certain whether you will be able to maintain the right position in the group if you remain completely true to yourself. What is fantastic about your developed egos is that you can also use them for the better, without fear motives, as an extension of your authenticity. If you have properly developed the Nice One, it is easier to manage people in a pleasant way from your own authenticity.

Sometimes you see egos form in managers who are assigned a lot of responsibility for the first time. As their new situation is different, a little unsafe, they are not certain whether they will be successful in their new role. Many managers use the egos they developed at the start of their career. These egos used to be successful, so why shouldn't they be called into play again? If, as a junior manager, you learned that you have to look up to directors and be very careful about delivering criticism if you want to make a career for yourself, you will later behave in the same way as a director towards the board (that is, if you are unable to keep your ego under control).

If you are repeatedly able to achieve the desired position by behaving in a certain way, an important story will be created in your inner world: 'If I want to get this or that out of someone else, I need to behave in this way or that way'. If you have repeated this thousands of times, the behaviour will have become an ingrained pattern, a success formula, a certain self-image. *An ego will have been formed.* You can call this ego into play whenever you want. An ego automatically (subconsciously) comes into play if a situation closely resembles a previous one when it was successful. You saw in Chapter 4 (norms) that you continually label your environment. Ego behaviour is often observed in people who are pressed up against the outer limit of their comfort zone, when a restrictive norm triggers an ego. No two comfort zones are the same, that is, a certain norm in your inner world about your environment brings out a specific ego. Your inner world is full of these tricks. Different egos are stored in your inner world to be called into play for different situations without you being aware of it. You should not see this as a bad thing instead you should embrace these egos as they can benefit you. However, don't let them get the better of you, otherwise things will go wrong.

ADVANTAGES AND DISADVANTAGES OF USING EGOS

Advantages

- Success is almost guaranteed. The good thing about egos is that they help you secure a desired position in a group. There are reasons that it has become a formula for success. Previously, an ego must have served you well; otherwise you wouldn't have developed it further. It gives you a good feeling to achieve a certain result in the group, even if the outcome was not achieved by your authentic self.

- Another advantage of egos is that they can immediately be called into play. They are always on hand to take over from your authentic self, if necessary.

- Your various egos have also taught you how to influence people. These skills can be used when you want to influence others from your authenticity (see Chapter 7).

- An ego is also referred to as a survival strategy. This indicates that egos help you survive in unsafe situations. If your environment does not feel safe to you (for example, when you notice that your position in the group is the subject of discussion), your ego immediately sets to work. The various egos which you have developed protect you. You could regard your egos as gatekeepers that protect your true self from disaster (see Figure 5.2).

Figure 5.2 Egos as gatekeepers

Disadvantages

Your egos have only one goal: to position themselves. The things I describe here are sometimes difficult to recognise. And if they are recognised, they are sometimes painful to acknowledge. This is why many people don't look for their egos. After all, it is not at all nice to realise that your exaggerated ego can often play up. Comfort yourself with the thought that by recognising a number of issues, you will clear the way for a deeper sense of fulfilment. But first you need to know what is holding you back. From being unconsciously incompetent (you're unaware that you're calling your egos into play) you become consciously incompetent (you're aware of occasionally making mistakes because of calling your egos into play). In Chapter 8 you will really set to work to become consciously more competent.

- The main idea behind using your egos is that you do your best to be labelled by others. You will feel satisfied when you have been labelled or have positioned yourself in a certain way, sometimes even happy. However, the question is 'Who actually determines your success or happiness?' Is it you or the other person? The answer is: the other person. You will not be satisfied until the other person makes the desired response to your behaviour. And that is the problem with egos – by calling your egos into play, you become, by definition, dependent on others, on your environment. Others, and not you, determine your happiness. It therefore takes a lot of energy to use egos. You are constantly manipulating your environment and seeking recognition. In fact, you are living from your outermost layer inwards, and that takes energy.

- If you often call your egos into play, you lose yourself a little. Something that was once used as a successful trick eventually becomes less successful because it may begin to show obsessive characteristics. There comes a time when your ego controls everything. The problem here is that you stop being aware of this. You will actually start to think that it is your authentic behaviour, while it has little to do with authenticity, since you are not creating; you are just positioning yourself. And you are not even positioning your true self, but your ego. When you call your ego into play obsessively, you will notice that this detracts from your sense of fulfilment, since even when you achieve results by calling your ego into play, deep down you feel that your false persona, and not you, has achieved these results. This makes you feel unreal, or empty. You feel dissatisfied. You start to ask yourself 'Is this the real me?' You may recognise these moments of self-reflection: you become aware that, although you've got everything your heart desires, you are still not very happy. When this happens, you're at a crossroads. A complicated crossroads, because you will probably come to the conclusion that you haven't been yourself for a very long time. You have become a walking ego.

- People will see through you at some point (sometimes sooner than you might expect), especially if you call the exaggerated variant of your ego into play. Many people, especially those with a high EQ or a lot of life experience, will feel that you are pulling a trick on them. They will feel manipulated, tricked by your ego; they will feel that they are being driven into a corner. They will feel that your behavioural intention is not directed at them but at yourself. Think of the manager who has been told to ask you about your proposal during a delegation skills course but who is really not interested in your proposal at all, as he has already made his own plans. Or perhaps you recognise the feeling that sneaks up on you when a consultant tells you one success story after another. You feel used, manipulated. You are, as it were, forced to give a certain response. If this feeling manifests itself in the other person, you will definitely not get the response you want. People don't accept being manipulated. You are therefore taking a significant risk of getting caught when you call your egos into play and your reputation or position in the group is particularly at risk.

- If you use your exaggerated ego too often, and the other person realises this, you will find that she will also use her exaggerated egos. After all, you call your ego into play in order to position yourself in relation to another person. Because the other person's position is under attack, she will use her egos to defend herself. It is just like two balloons in a shoebox; if one balloon is inflated, the other will immediately feel the pressure mount and react by applying counter-pressure. Therefore, you will not get to see the other person's true self. All deals that revolve round egos are vulnerable, as you will continue to ask yourself what the real, underlying motives were. Is this really what the other person wants, or is there a snake in the grass which you haven't seen yet? You run the risk of being manipulated yourself.

- A negative self-fulfilling prophecy is a major risk, as it is a threat to your effectiveness and happiness. Negative self-fulfilling prophecies only occur in the exaggerated variants of an ego. I have already pointed out that egos are often called into play when you experience your environment as unsafe. In such a case, your behaviour is driven by your fear motive. You start to avoid things and to compensate for things, while in the background this fear continues to be an important story in your inner world.

Now examine some of the propositions you have come across: (1) egos are often called into play in unsafe environments; (2) an unsafe environment is an environment where you think that your position in the group is the subject of discussion; (3) if your fears continue to drive your behaviour, they will, as a result of a negative self-fulfilling prophecy, eventually come true.

This last proposition can be expressed as:

Fear → Compensation → Short-term success → Overcompensation → Fears eventually become reality.

You compensate for fear by calling one of your egos into play.

These propositions are combined into a new one: if your fear of being in the wrong position in a group continues to drive your behaviour, your ego will eventually put you into this position as a result of a negative self-fulfilling prophecy. In other words, if you repeatedly call your egos into play over a long period of time, you run the risk that your fears will come true. Although your ego benefited you in the past, it will now take you down the wrong path. Egos help you in the short-term but work against you in the long-term (see Figure 5.3).

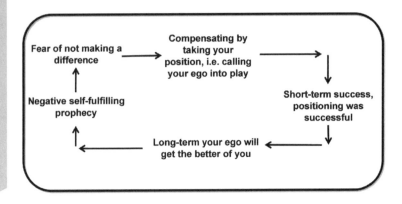

Figure 5.3 Negative self-fulfilling prophecy of an exaggerated ego in case of fear

When you call the exaggerated variant into play, the people around you will no longer see your beautiful 'deeper' self, your authenticity. People will actually start to believe this behaviour is your deepest self as your authenticity is obscured (see Figure 5.4).

Figure 5.4 Your authenticity becomes invisible

The advantages and disadvantages of calling egos into play should now be clear. The trick is to become aware of your egos and then to call them into play for strategic reasons or, conversely, to decide not to use them at all. This entails analysing the advantages and disadvantages in advance so that, in any case, you do not end up becoming the victim of your exaggerated egos. This is a good reason to take a closer look at our various egos.

EIGHT EGOS

Dozens of different egos can be identified and the different types have been discussed in various theoretical works. They sometimes go by different names, such as sub-personalities, survival strategies, coping strategies, preferred typologies. What is noteworthy is that some types are very similar, with the trick being to properly classify them. Because the use of an ego is a matter of positioning in this book, I have distinguished the eight egos in terms of the position they aim to achieve in relation to another person. You will notice that this classification is as simple as it is practical.

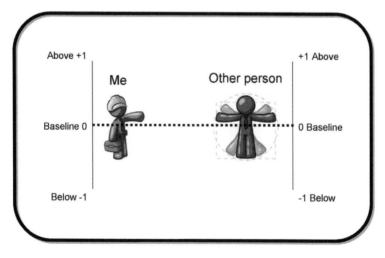

Figure 5.5 Three positions: above, alongside or below another person

You can position yourself in three different ways in relation to another person (your environment): above the person (+1), alongside the person (0) or below the person (-1) (see Figure 5.5). So, if someone is, so to speak, worth a 9, and you are also worth a 9, then the relative score is 0:0. We call the zero line the baseline.

In the discussion below you will see that all egos will want to reposition you in a certain way in relation to another person. I give egos two different names: the successful variant, the strength of an ego (in case of Ego 1, this is the Proud One) and the exaggerated, unsuccessful variant, which results in a negative self-fulfilling prophecy (in the case of Ego 1, this is the Show-off).

When I describe the egos, I classify them according to objective, behaviour, potential fears and negative self-fulfilling prophecy. I illustrate each ego with a practical example and discuss the difference between calling your ego into play based on your creation motive and calling your ego into play based on your fear motive.

Ego 1: The Proud One, the Show-off

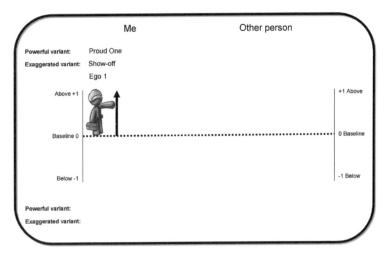

Figure 5.6 The Proud One, the Show-off

I recently came across the following quote in a professional journal: 'You know, lay-offs come with the territory. They're hard, but just have to be done. You have to be up to it, otherwise you should choose a different line of work.'

- *Powerful variant:* the Proud One

- *Exaggerated variant:* the Show-off

- *Desired position*: +1 (top position in the group).

- *The Proud One moves:* from 0 to +1.

- *Objective*: to be admired.

- *Behaviour*: you want to acquire status by showing the other person how good you are.

- *Potential fears*: not being admired.

- *Potential negative self-fulfilling prophecy*: people don't admire you because they think you're a show-off.

- *Other types falling under this ego*: the He-Man, the Macho Man, Mr Know-It-All, the Know-All, the Braggart.

When you call this ego into play, you are trying to elevate yourself to a higher level. You are very proud of yourself. You are not really focused on others. In meetings, you always manage to refer to successful cases you were involved in. You show that you actually know more about everything and do everything better than others. You do most of the talking during meetings, which makes you feel very pleased with yourself. The good thing about this ego is that there's nothing wrong with being proud of yourself. In fact, you should be happy if you are proud of yourself. False modesty often qualifies as ego behaviour. However, it does make a big difference if you are proud because you are genuinely good or because you just want to be thought of as good.

Example

The quarterly results are discussed during a meeting. The marketing director points out that the good results were actually achieved through his insights and efforts: 'We had a very hard time getting sales back on track after the merger. Fortunately, I had dealt with this before. I could tell that people were not motivated. I immediately called the team of sales managers together and explained how they could motivate their account managers in these new situations and monitor their targets more closely. Things are back to normal, as you can tell from the scores.'

Desired response: 'Gosh, you're good …!'

Based on the creation motive

By positioning yourself as a Proud One, you receive attention. You are able to share the enjoyment of your beautiful creations with others and achieve notice as a result. You may be assigned more responsibilities. You will be able to make an even bigger contribution to the team in the future. You also set the right example for others, so they don't have to make themselves smaller than they are.

Based on the fear motive

As the Proud One or Show-off you talk a lot about yourself, probably because you feel a need to. You probably want to prevent people thinking less of you or not taking you seriously if you don't. When this happens, you find yourself a little excluded from the group. So you blow your own trumpet. Well, if I don't, who will?!

Negative self-fulfilling prophecy in case of the exaggerated variant

There comes a time when people get tired of all your self-glorification. It's fine to be proud of yourself, but telling others how good you are all the time is called showing off. And that's annoying. Because of all this mindless talk about yourself, you don't allow others to speak. People sense this. They will quickly pass you over and no longer take your stories seriously. It may even raise a few sniggers in the corridors. 'Oh him … yes, he's very pleased with himself,' they tell each other with a wink. So, when you, the Proud One, really achieve something, it won't be recognised ('It's probably another of his tall stories …'). Lo and behold, your fears come true. The Proud One is no longer admired and the group sidelines him.

Sound familiar? 'Look Mum, look what I can do!'

Ego 2: The Independent One, the Soloist

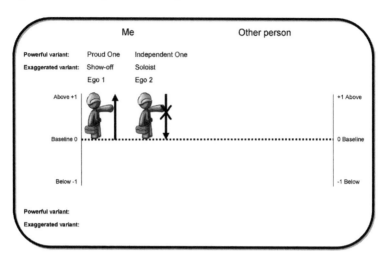

Figure 5.7 The Independent One, the Soloist

'If I were to need coaching, to me that would mean that I'm not up to the job and I would then have to draw my conclusions …'

- *Powerful variant:* the Independent One

- *Exaggerated variant:* the Soloist

- *Desired position:* +1 (top position in the group).

- *The Independent One makes the following move:* hold on to the +1.

- *Objective:* to retain the admiration of others.

- *Behaviour:* showing others, implicitly and explicitly, that you can do it yourself, that you don't need any support or advice, that you would rather not interact with others.

- *Potential fears:* losing your elevated position in the group (and, as a result, status).

- *Potential negative self-fulfilling prophecy:* you are not admired because people think you're too much of a soloist.

- *Other types falling under this ego:* the Lone Wolf, the Best.

When you call this ego into play, you are trying to maintain your high-level position. You *don't* want to interact with others. You can do it all by yourself. You turn down offers of assistance. You achieve good results that you can be proud of by yourself. You don't need to lean on others. You have always managed on your own, so why involve others? You only call in others to have things done for you. Independence is a very good quality. However, it makes a big difference whether you are independent because you can actually do everything better than everyone else, or because you want people to think that you can.

Example

The general manager sees that the director of operations is having difficulty getting his business unit's primary process back on track. The merger is costing him a lot of energy. The general manager offers to make time to jointly investigate the problems. To which the director of operations replies: 'No, thanks. Fortunately, that's really not necessary. I can manage on my own.'

Desired response: 'He's so independent. He'll be okay. Quite impressive ...'

Based on the creation motive

It is a good quality when people are able to take things on independently. You sometimes get things done slightly faster when you do them yourself. It also makes people look up to you when you handle everything by yourself and never ask for or accept help. Some people could benefit from following this example.

Based on the fear motive

As the Independent One or the Soloist, you don't want your image to be damaged by having to admit that you could use some help. You don't want people to think that you *can't* do it all by yourself, because they might see this as a sign of weakness. If you accept help, you think that you are making yourself dependent on others. This is a common restrictive norm. Therefore, in your perception, your interaction with others actually forms a threat to your position in the group.

Negative self-fulfilling prophecy under the exaggerated variant
Being independent is an essential quality for all leaders. It wouldn't be good if you needed assistance with everything. A negative self-fulfilling prophecy can only take place in the long-term if the Independent One becomes the Soloist. This can happen in two different ways. Firstly, because you never ask for help, your results may not be as good as they should be and you therefore lose respect. Secondly (and in practice this is more common), you will lose your elevated position because others will think that you go it alone too often. 'You can't work with him, so just pass him over.' In both cases, your fears become reality and you lose your elevated position.

Sound familiar? 'I want to do it myself …'

Ego 3: The Defender, the Victim

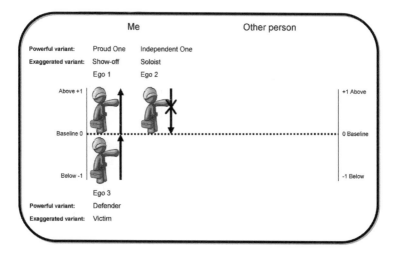

Figure 5.8 The Defender, the Victim

'I wasn't able to turn the company around because the unions wouldn't cooperate …'

- *Powerful variant:* the Defender

- *Exaggerated variant:* the Victim

- *Desired position*: 0.

- *The Defender moves:* from -1 to 0.

- *Objective*: to defend yourself, not to be held accountable or found guilty, to stand up for yourself when you are criticised, to receive compassion and sympathy.

- *Behaviour*: telling others that you're not responsible for the situation that has arisen, placing the responsibility with others, setting limits, telling others that you've got it very hard, complaining.

- *Potential fears*: being rejected because you are guilty or held responsible for a bad situation.

- *Potential negative self-fulfilling prophecy*: you are rejected because all you do is complain, because you don't take responsibility and because people are tired of you playing the victim.

- *Other types falling under this ego*: the Complainer, the Moaner, the Warner.

It is good to defend yourself or your team. It is also good to put forward sound reasons for why a responsibility should not be placed with you if it rightly belongs with someone else. It is good to point out why things are not going the way they should and use that information to decide on a course of action. It is also good to refuse to allow too many tasks and responsibilities to be pushed onto your plate and to set limits. You are quite right to do so in order to get yourself out of a relatively weak position, or not to get into that position in the first place. You do this by pointing out that you've got it very hard, that you are incredibly busy, have loads to do, or that the bad situation should actually be attributed to others. You are not to blame, are not responsible, you can't do anything about it. It is sometimes nice to receive support or compassion. In any case, you want the other person to elevate you from -1 back to 0. You don't want to be held responsible for the -1 position. However, it does make a difference whether you defend yourself justifiably or whether you only want to be seen to be blameless.

Example

The general manager asks the IT director why the IT expenses are still not in line with the budget despite what was agreed. The IT director replies: 'Currently I have more executive vacancies open than before. I am putting in twelve-hour days. I always said the budget would come under pressure. The merger was simply ill-timed.'

Desired response: 'Yes, you're right, there's nothing you could have done about it. You're handling everything fine. I won't bother you about this again.'

Based on the creation motive

You want to place the responsibility where it belongs. You set limits on what you do and do not want to do. Others should also take responsibility. In this way, you will receive the understanding and support you need. And, in so doing, you create room to address the things that do fall under your responsibility.

Based on the fear motive

As the Defender or the Victim, you want to prevent the loss of your position in the group because you are not functioning properly. It is clear that you are in a -1 position, as things are not going the way they should do. You're being watched, others are possibly not happy with you, nor is it likely that they will become happier with you. Although you could assume responsibility, you don't want things to go wrong, because then you would definitely lose your position.

Negative self-fulfilling prophecy under the exaggerated variant

In the long-term the negative self-fulfilling prophecy can take place in two different ways. Firstly, people are simply fed up with the fact that the problem hasn't gone away; if the problem grows, you will eventually lose your position as the Defender, whether you can do anything about it or not. Secondly, people are tired of you complaining and playing the victim. In Chapter 2 you saw the negative consequences of too much complaining. The point is that others think that you *ought* to assume responsibility. Stop moaning, do something about it! A Complainer will eventually be cast aside as a moaner.

Sound familiar? 'I didn't do it!'

Ego 4: The Quiet One, the Dodger

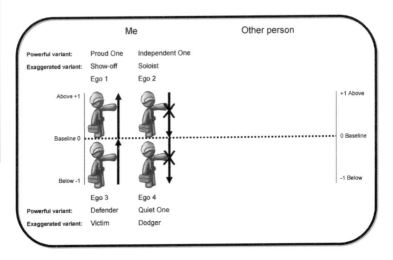

Figure 5.9 The Quiet One, the Dodger

'Heads down and lie low when you're under fire ...'

- *Powerful variant:* the Quiet One

- *Exaggerated variant:* the Dodger

- *Desired position:* 0.

- *The Quiet One makes the following move:* hold on to the 0.

- Objective: to be left alone, to avoid attracting attention in order to avoid failure.

- *Behaviour:* avoids contact by not attracting attention, by not being burdened and by not risking upsetting the working relationship.

- *Potential fears:* failure, and therefore being thrown out of the group.

- *Potential negative self-fulfilling prophecy:* others think that you have failed because you aren't contributing anything, so you lose your position and are thrown out of the group.

- *Other types falling under this ego:* the Quiet One, the Invisible One, the Avoider, the Anxious Performer.

This ego slightly resembles Ego 2 (the Independent One), since you would rather not interact with others. And here that is also a good quality because you give others space and do not react impulsively. First you observe and analyse. The difference with the Independent One is that, as a Quiet One, you don't position yourself at the top. Your aim is to avoid attracting attention rather than to maintain high status. By avoiding contact, you also avoid situations you can't handle. New situations may seem threatening. However, you are also afraid to give your informed opinion or feedforward because you don't want to risk disrupting your working relationships. Nevertheless, when you do interact with others, you find it difficult to say 'no' because you worry that others will feel let down by you, or think that you are not pulling your weight. There is a difference between 'being calm' and 'avoiding contact'.

Example

The HR officer notes that the IT director hasn't got it completely right – there are now fewer executive vacancies than there were four months ago. The HR officer decides to say nothing.

Desired response: None really. The HR officer is not seen or heard, so no response will be made.

Based on the creation motive

It is wise to test the waters before reacting. You don't have to react to everything. Choose your battles. This will allow you to add more value when you do communicate something. Moreover, it is good to give others some space.

Based on the fear motive

As the Quiet One or the Invisible One, you want to avoid making mistakes, to prevent conflicts, and avoid becoming the focus of attention. Your hope is that your position in the group will not become the subject of discussion. A Quiet One will recognise the feeling that sneaks up on you when, for example, you attend a networking meeting and don't know anyone there. You worry that everyone is watching you and can sense your insecurity. You wish you could be invisible.

Negative self-fulfilling prophecy under the exaggerated variant

It is obvious that a negative self-fulfilling prophecy will eventually occur. If you never make a contribution because you are afraid of failure, you will fail in the working relationship as you don't add any value. People will accuse you of elusive behaviour, of never taking responsibility or initiative and of never confronting others. This will put your position in the group at risk. Alternatively, you could become so good at ducking your head that you won't be seen and won't be taken into account any more. Your role has simply been played out.

Sound familiar? The fear of giving presentations? Or the deadly silence when your mother asked who would put out the rubbish bins?

EGOS TARGETING OTHERS

The four egos I have just discussed are not really focused on the other person. They are largely preoccupied with themselves and their own position, rather than with changing the other person's position:

- The Proud One only talks about himself.

- The Independent One and the Quiet One don't want to have any contact with others.

- The Defender just says he's not to blame, irrespective of the other person's position.

In the following four egos, you will see that the behaviour is specifically targeted at the other person. The aim is to change the other person's position in order to obtain a relatively better position for oneself.

Ego 5: The Nice One, the Sweet Talker

'We are hugely impressed by the creativity and entrepreneurship of the intermediaries. That is why we like to do business with them.'

- *Powerful variant:* The Nice One

- *Exaggerated variant:* the Sweet Talker

- *Desired position*: one step up.

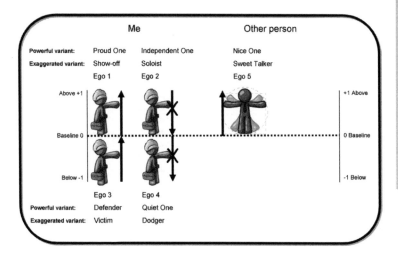

Figure 5.10 The Nice One, the Sweet Talker

- *The Nice One makes the following move*: The Nice One hopes that, by elevating the other person from 0 to +1, the other person will also elevate him (from -1 to 0 or from 0 to +1).

- *Objective*: to regain recognition and be part of the group.

- *Behaviour*: showing appreciation of or entertaining the other person.

- *Potential fears*: not receiving recognition and not being allowed to be part of the group.

- *Potential negative self-fulfilling prophecy*: people thinking that you no longer fit in because they're tired of your sweet-talking.

- *Other types falling under this ego*: the Clown, Prince Charming, the Love Junkie, the Groveller, the Pleaser.

The Nice One tries to put someone else on a pedestal. By entertaining others, by making them laugh or by telling them how good or beautiful they are, you can make others feel good. That is a nice thing to do and people will like you as a result. The question is whether you are really nice, or whether you simply want to be liked. It may actually not be the Nice One's intention to make others feel good. He may simply want to be rewarded for this behaviour, that is, he is really just fishing for compliments. In terms of positioning, this means you will move up a step. This ego can take on many different guises. The simplest guises are those of the Complimenter, the Groveller and Prince Charming. This ego also manifests itself as a clown. By making others laugh, you hope to strengthen your position. You are often laughing off problems when you do so. The Nice One sometimes resembles the Quiet One, since he also avoids conflicts. The difference is that, while the Quiet One avoids taking the initiative, you, the Nice One, takes the initiative to improve a relationship.

Example

The IT director discovers that he has insufficient testing capacity. He simply forgot to plan for this. The people who can help him out are in the operations department. He turns to the director of operations: 'Pretty good, the way you were able to land those first-rate recruits as it's quite difficult to find good employees these days. I understand you also took over a few strong employees from our merger partner. I think my team could learn a lot from yours. Do you think you could transfer two staff members to my department on a secondment basis?'

Desired response: 'He's a nice guy. I'll do him a favour …'

Based on the creation motive

Making people feel good about themselves helps people to develop further and strengthens relationships. It motivates people to do things for you because they like you. You keep people on the ball in a pleasant way. You also receive the recognition you deserve. You make easy contact with new people because you put them in the spotlight.

Based on the fear motive

As the Nice One or the Sweet Talker, you want to avoid being left out. You continually want to receive compliments, or confirmation that you are an esteemed member of the group. But unfortunately, when you do receive such confirmation your sense of satisfaction does not last very long.

Negative self-fulfilling prophecy under the exaggerated variant

At some point people grow tired of the endless joking, the flattery, the fact that you are always afraid to get into a heavy discussion. People start to think you're a sweet talker. They feel that they have been taken advantage of, or that your added value amounts to nothing. They will therefore throw you out of the group, or you will no longer receive recognition. Your fears have come true and the negative self-fulfilling prophecy is fulfilled.

Sound familiar? 'You're my best friend. Am I yours?'

Ego 6: The Relativist, the Envious One

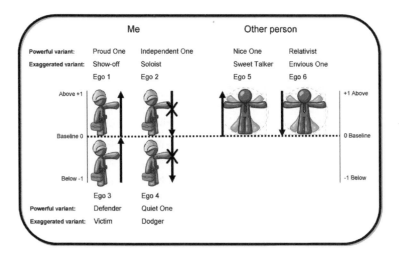

Figure 5.11 The Relativist, the Envious One

'The success of this particular competitor has more to do with the favourable economic conditions than with her own qualities.'

- *Powerful variant:* the Relativist

- *Exaggerated variant:* the Envious One

- *Desired position:* one step up.

- *The* Relativist *makes the following move*: by displacing the other person from +1 to 0, he moves up in relation to this person (from -1 to 0 or from 0 to +1).

- *Objective*: for the other person to be demoted so that you can move up in relation to their fall.

- *Behaviour*: downplaying the success of others.

- *Potential fears*: receiving less recognition yourself.

- *Potential negative self-fulfilling prophecy*: people do not give you as much recognition because they recognise your jealous behaviour.

- *Other types falling under this ego*: the Jealous One, the Best, Mr Know-It-All, the Cynic, the Aggrieved One, the Downplayer.

The Relativist tries to pull someone else off her pedestal because he doesn't want to let the success of others distract from his success. It is a good thing to believe in your own strengths. That is what you should focus on. However, there is a difference between putting success into perspective and jealous behaviour based on the idea that the success of another could be a personal threat. You believe that if someone else receives attention, you will miss out on recognition (that you do make a difference). To solve this problem, you move up in relation to others by bringing them down. The other person's success is put down to luck, or external circumstances. You sometimes try to claim another's success for yourself by suggesting that it's because of you that the other person is successful. You usually come across the Relativist in competitive environments, where there is really only room for one at the top. As a client, you notice this when suppliers start talking about other suppliers. In companies, you come across jealous behaviour when a position becomes available. To put it simply, this kind of behaviour is 'pulling the rug from under somebody else's feet'. This is sometimes successful, but can also lead to your own downfall.

Example
The marketing director is listening to the sales director's boastful talk in a meeting. There has been a conflict of interests between the marketing

and sales departments for some time now. Who actually sets the policy? Marketing or sales? The marketing director is annoyed by the sales director's smug explanation as it does not look good for his own position. He wonders how he can bring the other person down subtly. He says 'I see that the sales figures have actually gone up. That's great, but I also see that costs have increased dramatically. How does that work in relation to the return objectives?'

Desired response: 'The sales director's success is not that impressive after all …'

Based on the creation motive

Believe in your own strengths and don't let yourself be distracted by the success of others. They have their own problems. If you stop focusing on others, your own activities and successes will once again become the focus of your attention. It helps to prevent panic among your own team members when you tell them that your growth does not depend on comparison with a successful competitor and allows them to believe in their own successes again.

Based on the fear motive

As the Relativist or the Envious One, you want to prevent others from receiving too much attention and recognition, which you believe means that you receive less attention and recognition. You therefore put the success of others into perspective. Negatively put, you are slightly jealous. The other person is taking the limelight away from you. You want to be recognised for what you do. You're afraid others have achieved success at your expense and that you will therefore lose your position in the group. This Relativist reaction is one of the reasons why people make themselves smaller than they really are. After all, by 'being your true self' you run the risk that the Relativist will bring you down and dismiss your success as hot air.

Negative self-fulfilling prophecy under the exaggerated variant

In the short-term you might succeed in reinforcing your position by bringing others down. However, the victim of this action will hold it against you and may start to call her own egos into play in order to bring you down. Two egos will clash, subtly or otherwise. Your actions as the Envious One are not necessarily always targeted at the person who is in position +1. You often share your observations with others in order to cloud their perception of the 'successful' fellow group member. People will see through this at some point. They will recognise your bad behaviour. When this happens, they will immediately lower your position. Their trust in you is diminished, since you could just as easily direct your actions at them. You fall in their esteem and therefore lose your position. Your fears have become reality and the *negative* self-fulfilling prophecy is fulfilled.

Sound familiar? When you were a child, did you and your friends gossip about a popular friend who got all the attention, behind her back?

Ego 7: The Adviser, the Paternalist

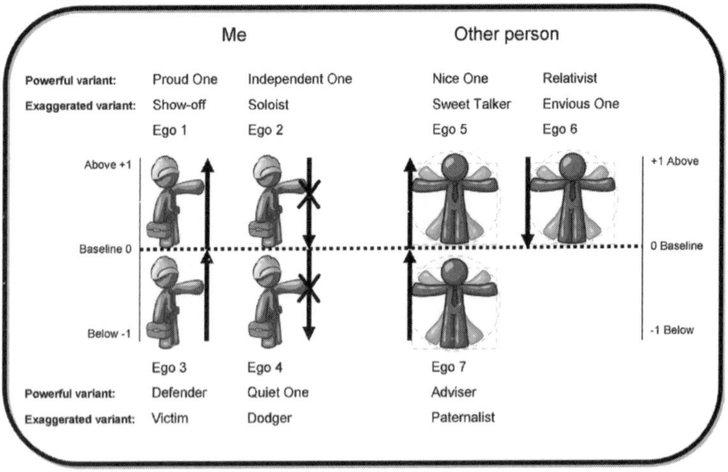

Figure 5.12 The Adviser, the Paternalist

A coach reported 'All managers should engage a coach, because they need someone who helps them solve their problems.'

• *Powerful variant:* the Adviser

• *Exaggerated variant:* the Paternalist

- *Desired position*: one step up.

- *The Adviser makes the following move*: by elevating the other person from -1 to 0, he himself moves up from 0 to +1.

- *Objective*: to make himself indispensable by helping others, thereby positioning himself above the others, gratitude, to make others dependent on him.

- *Behaviour*: advising or trying to save others.

- *Potential fears*: not being indispensable.

- *Potential negative self-fulfilling prophecy*: others no longer need you because they feel that they are continually forced into an underdog position or because they are annoyed by your paternalistic behaviour.

- *Other types falling under this ego*: the Helper, the Saviour, the Best, Mr Know-It-All, the Warner, the Know-All, the Indispensable One, Mother Hen.

As an Adviser you position yourself as *the* person who is needed to help someone out of a predicament. This is a very good quality in itself. It even looks very authentic to elevate people to a higher level and you receive recognition for assisting in someone's development. However, the question is whether you do this because you want to help others (develop further) or because you want to position yourself. Your aim may not be to help others, but to receive recognition and an elevated position in return. You simply have to be 'indispensable'. In that case, your help is not unconditional. You position yourself above the person you're trying to help. You tend to look for problems in others, since that gives you the opportunity to come to the rescue. You have to be indispensable to others in order to keep your position in the group. You can be recognised as an Adviser because you want to advise others on how to do nearly everything more effectively or differently, whether this concerns management, renovating a house, dealing with children or their holiday destination.

Example

The general manager sees that the director of operations is finding it difficult to get his business unit's primary process back on track. The general manager has felt for a while that his team members don't need him. They have become very independent during the merger period. He has taken a step back from heading up the management team because he has spent most of his time lately consulting with the unions and works councils. The implementation of the new structure and the related adjustments to the primary processes were largely handled by steering committees. For practical reasons, these steering committees were mostly chaired by other directors. The merger has now been finalised and because things are slowly getting back to normal, the general manager is able to concentrate on heading up the management team. However, he wonders if his colleagues actually still need him and therefore offers to make time to help the director of operations. He wants to be needed.

Desired response: 'I really appreciate your help. I do in fact need you ...'

Based on the creation motive

It is great to be able to assist and advise others and to see their development. People like to be around you, they learn from you and need you. You are always prepared to spend time and energy on others. Because they come straight to you when they need help, you are a highly esteemed team member.

Based on the fear motive

As the Adviser or Paternalist you want to avoid becoming dispensable. If you are unable to give advice, you will lose your raison d'être. No matter how good people are, you simply have to find that one thing that still requires some work, otherwise you will no longer be needed.

Negative self-fulfilling prophecy under the exaggerated variant

In the short-term you manage to get the recognition from others for the help you provide. However, there are two risk factors for a negative self-fulfilling prophecy. In the first place, it is impossible to know everything about everything. You are sometimes inclined to give advice on matters of which you have no knowledge. In doing so, you quickly lose the respect of others and they no longer ask for your help. 'After all, who are you to advise me?!' In the second place, people eventually find it annoying when they are not given the chance to deal with their own problems. They will start accusing you of being paternalistic and feel that you are trying to make others dependent on you and so start to avoid you. Your fears are confirmed. You are no longer needed. Your role has been played out.

Sound familiar? 'Shall I carry your books?'

Ego 8: The Powerful One, the Demolisher

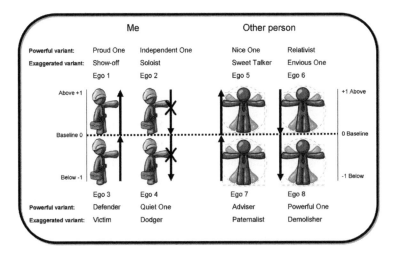

Figure 5.13 The Powerful One, the Demolisher

'If they won't give in to our demands now, we will close the place down.'

- *Powerful variant:* the Powerful One

- *Exaggerated variant:* the Demolisher

- *Desired position:* one step up.

- *The Powerful One makes the following move:* displacing someone else from 0 to -1 to automatically position himself above the other person.

- *Objective*: to be the boss, to win, to command respect, to dominate others.

- *Behaviour*: imposing his will by pulling others down and threatening them.

- *Potential fears*: that people won't respect you(r) (opinion).

- *Potential negative self-fulfilling prophecy*: people don't really respect you because they are afraid of you and/or think your behaviour is disrespectful.

- *Other types falling under this ego*: the Cynic, the Impetuous Child, the Demander, the Threatener, the Wrecker.

On the one hand, it is a good quality to be able to exude strength as a leader. It provides clarity, for example, about the course of action to be followed. Decisions need to be made. It is not bedlam, a company is not a democracy. It is wonderful to follow a strong leader in times of crisis. He knows what is good for you. The question is whether you are strong or just want to be thought of as strong. In the negative variant, you try to eliminate others (and their creativity), that is, to 'demolish'. This is not about how clear an intended strategy or course of action is, but your own position. 'I'm the boss, and whoever crosses me will be sorry.' You act forcefully to get your own way or command respect. People should be a little afraid of you. 'Do this, otherwise …' You silence others and threaten them when they don't do what you want them to do. These threats could mean that others are irked by you, or that you have directly engaged their fear motives and they are concerned about the unwanted consequences of crossing you. The Demolisher resembles the Envious One since both of them try to lower the other person's position. The difference with the Envious One is that he wants to dethrone someone (from +1 to 0) while the Powerful One or Demolisher knocks the other person under the baseline (to -1).

Example

The marketing director has just tried to deflate the sales director by in-quiring after his department's return on sales. The sales director isn't going to put up with such an attack on his position and responds 'It's rather curious that you, of all people, are inquiring about our return on sales. If there's one unit that ought to be questioning its return on sales, it's the marketing department.'

Desired response: 'I have to watch out for him.'

Based on the creation motive

It's good to show your strength. You really want to create things and this sometimes calls for clarity. No false modesty, but taking responsibility for making decisions. If others don't want to, then that's too bad, it just has to be done. You keep others on course. You command respect by taking firm action. At least you're not afraid. You call others to account. You force others to leave their comfort zone.

Based on the fear motive

As the Powerful One or the Demolisher, you want to avoid losing authority or power by failing to position yourself above others. They mustn't contradict you, because if they're right, you will lose your reputation and, as a result, your position. They mustn't question your self-confidence, because in reality, you might not be all that confident. You must hide your fears.

Negative self-fulfilling prophecy under the exaggerated variant

As the Powerful One, you are usually very effective in the shorter term. You know how to overwhelm others in such a way that they put up little resistance. They don't want to engage with you (yet). In the longer term they will lose respect for you, despite the fact that you repeatedly try to command it. Others might even become slightly afraid of you. This negative self-fulfilling prophecy can be fulfilled in a number of different ways. Firstly, people may let you have your way, not so much because they respect you as a human being (as they actually think you're a very bad colleague), but because they want to put an end to your dominant behaviour as quickly as possible. But they will not go the extra mile for you. Secondly, others may start to defend themselves against you, sometimes jointly. The infighting becomes increasingly intense, especially when several people clash at the same time. You may lose the battle and have to leave the field. Or people may turn away from you, leaving you all by yourself. Either way, you lose respect.

Sound familiar? 'If you do that one more time…'

EGO POSITIONING

There are many other types apart from these eight egos. You will come across some of these types in several egos. For example, you will come across Mr Know-It-All in the Proud One, the Relativist and the Adviser. This ego can be used for different positions. Another example is the Perfectionist, an ego which, to some extent, we can all relate to. The question is 'What move does the Perfectionist want to make?' As the Proud One (to be admired), as the Independent One (to stay on his pedestal), or as the Quiet One (to not fail)? All of these are possible. If you come across other egos you would like to examine further, it will help you to find out what move they are trying to make. The fear and negative self-fulfilling prophecy will be identical to those of one of the eight egos that are trying to make the same move. The egos and their various characteristics are summarised in a table in Appendix 2.

HOW ARE WE USING EGOS?

The process by which you come to your behaviour was described in Chapter 2. The manner in which the same process works when egos are called into play is described below.

Selective perception This starts with selectively perceiving an event in your environment. You perceive events that have to do with your position.

The association process You ask yourself where you have come across this before, scanning your inner world in order to identify similar stories.

The evaluation process You ask yourself three questions:

1. *How should I label this information?* Is the information threatening or safe? You ask yourself what the situation means for your position. Can I be myself or should I use a trick? So, you see that a norm (layer 4)

brings out an ego. If you could label your environment differently, this would affect the use of your egos.

2. *What potential consequences will this have?* For example, ask yourself which of the other person's responses you value the most. This could stem from either the creation or fear motive. In case of the creation motive, you want to realise a desired consequence (e.g. admiration by others). In case of the fear motive, you may try to prevent an undesired consequence (e.g. losing the admiration of others).

3. *What are the potential courses of action?* What produces the greatest rewards? If you feel that your environment is not safe, you will decide during this part of the evaluation process which of the egos stored in your inner world will best help you to elicit a certain response from the other person. You are in fact setting the ego that will produce the best results as the norm.

Behaviour Once you have made your choice, you will display your 'old' ego behaviour by using your skills.

You are usually not aware of this process. It is a matter of trying to grasp it, of becoming aware of it, so that you can make a more conscious choice as to whether you call your ego into play or not. If you manage to perceive your environment as 'safe' (e.g. by paying more attention to the opportunities than to the threats), you will find that you will not call your egos into play as much as before (see Chapter 8).

TRY THIS...

- Look at the scores for your ego scan. If you are convinced that other egos are more dominant after reading their descriptions, you may want to adjust your scores. I emphasise again that everyone has all the egos discussed above. This scan is only intended to determine which egos you use the most.

- What decisions did you make last week based on your ego?

Try to find out which potential fears formed the basis for using these egos. Also try to find out which negative self-fulfilling prophecy could have troubled you.

- Next week, try to identify exaggerated egos in the people around you. Then try to find out which potential fears underlie the use of these egos. If you see that someone is troubled by her egos, you may want to try to help her remove the fears so that she will no longer have to use her egos.

AN IN-DEPTH PERSPECTIVE

Three ways of calling egos into play

You have already seen that egos can be used in different ways. Do you always call your egos into play? Yes, you always call your egos into play, although sometimes you make little use of them. Your ego is a way to position yourself. In other words, it is a way to attract attention, a way to interact with others. The egos you have developed form part of your character. They have helped shape your identity and are therefore useful systems, since you want to get your message across properly when communicating with others, even when you are not at all concerned with your position in the group. You use your specific strategies: whether you remain calm (the Quiet One), are humorous (the Nice One), are direct (the Powerful One), are supportive (the Adviser) or in whatever other way. Even when you help others to improve themselves from your authenticity, your egos will help you to make the impact you have in mind. Egos can be used in three different ways:

1. Based on your creation motive (authenticity). The growth of your environment is the determining factor here. Your ego helps you to make an impact. This is good, let it be, it works. You use the powerful variant here.

2. Based on your fear motive. Your position is under pressure, so you start to compensate by letting your ego take over. Fine. However,

you will add less value, since you run the risk that others will not recognise your creation motive. You use your powerful variant here. Be careful though, since your fear motive may (subconsciously) lead you to let your exaggerated variant get the better of you.

3. Exaggerated variant. This is where things go wrong. Make it a priority to learn to recognise this quickly and do not use it. The dynamic process turns against you. You end up in a negative self-fulfilling prophecy; your fear of losing your position comes true, people start to react from their own exaggerated variant because they know that your intentions are strictly focused on your own position.

Natural allergies between egos

When the various egos were discussed, you may have noticed that you found some egos to be more, or less, annoying. We all have allergies to the egos of others. This only happens in the *exaggerated variants*, which leads to something interesting: *the exaggerated variants* actually *trigger each other*. This means that your allergy for another person's ego triggers your exaggerated variant, and that in turn, your exaggerated variant can also provoke an allergic reaction in her, upon which she calls her exaggerated ego into play. An example is a Demolisher who is allergic to Victims. You might be able to imagine the following exchange:

Demolisher: 'Come on, take responsibility and stop moaning!'

Victim: 'Now you're just being nasty.'

Demolisher: 'Are you just going to keep on whining?'

In our experience, most problems in team-building and conflict mediation can be attributed to this. Many team disputes are fought out using substantive arguments (skills, knowledge and expertise), while the disputes actually take place on a deeper layer: restrictive norms that trigger exaggerated egos. It is sometimes like watching a table tennis game and you can almost predict who will react to someone's exaggerated variant. It is therefore useful to examine both your exaggerated variants and allergies. For us, it is, in addition to defining an inspiring mission (Chapter 7), a key to success in helping teams perform more effectively.

We often come across the following natural allergic reactions in practice:

- Ego 1 (the Show-off) and Ego 6 (the Envious One). The Show-off tries to put himself on a pedestal, but the Envious One almost immediately tries to knock him off again, pushing the Show-off to show off even more.

- Ego 2 (the Soloist) and Ego 7 (the Paternalist). The Soloist wants to do everything on her own without any help, while the Paternalist tries to find helpful things to do.

- Ego 3 (the Victim) and Ego 8 (the Demolisher). The Victim claims that others are to blame, while the Demolisher keeps on pointing out his responsibilities to him.

- Ego 5 (the Sweet Talker) and Ego 4 (the Dodger). The Dodger wants to be invisible, but the Sweet Talker continually puts her in the spotlight.

Once again, these are natural allergies. Apart from these allergies, various other combinations are possible. Although you come across this pattern in the slightly more extensive Ego Scans© that we ask team members to do, all kinds of other allergy combinations are possible. These allergies often result from specific restrictive norms that are prevalent in teams. The art is to raise this subject with a team or organisation without making a big thing out of it; egos are a fact of life, they benefit you, but you should not let them get the better of you. Can you imagine how nice it would be if two directors were to discuss their egos with one another? It would save a lot of trouble in the future.

A sample Ego Scan© of a manager and a sample Ego Scan© of his team are included in Appendix 3. These scans clearly show where the strength of the collaboration lies and where problems may arise. They show the powerful egos, the exaggerated variants that can result in a negative self-fulfilling prophecy (NSFP) and the allergies for the exaggerated variants of others.

Can egos make use of intermediaries?

The person on whom your ego is focused does not always have to label you in a certain way. Your ego could very well aim to influence a third person. You can recognise this in, for example, the Envious One. You focus your energies on the other person in order to pull a third person off his pedestal. For example, imagine our marketing director were to take the general manager aside to point out that the sales director's costs are going through the roof. In doing this he hopes the general manager will confront the sales director. The general manager is then used as an intermediary to pull the sales director off his pedestal. Mission accomplished. These are Machiavellian techniques and it is now popular to learn to use them. You will surely recognise how well or subtly some people have mastered them, but they can also be dangerous. If you respond in kind in order to defend yourself, you may find that you eventually fall victim to the unsafe situation you have created.

Being taken advantage of

It is useful to realise the risk you run of being taken advantage of when your own ego plays up.

- *Ego 1* (The Proud One) wants to acquire status. Another person can take advantage of this need by showing respect and giving praise, on the condition that the Proud One offers something in return.

- *Ego 2* (the Independent One) can be taken advantage of because things are arranged without involving her as she does not want to work with others anyway. As a result, the Independent One becomes isolated, has less power and starts to work harder and harder.

- *Ego 3* (the Defender) does not want to be held responsible. Someone else could take advantage of this need by feigning compassion, or by joining in with his complaining, on condition that the Defender arranges something for him.

- *Ego 4* (the Quiet One) can be taken advantage of because things are arranged without involving her, or by overloading her with work as the Quiet One will not say 'no'.

- *Ego 5* (The Nice One) can be taken advantage of by praising him to the skies.

- *Ego 6* (the Relativist) can be blackmailed with the fact that she tries to undermine others surreptitiously. She can also be incited to express her complaints to the person she believes has been put on a pedestal undeservedly, possibly with adverse consequences.

- *Ego 7* (the Adviser) can be taken advantage of by making excessive use of his services, by telling him that he is the saviour, with the result that the Adviser not only gives advice, but then also has to carry out all kinds of additional work.

- *Ego 8* (the Powerful One) can be taken advantage of by pointing out to her, supposedly in confidence, that there are people who want to undermine her power. The Demolisher will immediately counter-attack.

In summary, you could say that egos can not only benefit you, but that they can also benefit others who want to take advantage of you.

Labelling yourself in a certain way

Peter has been signed off work due to stress. He has gone through a very difficult period recently. Because of under-staffing, he has had to put in extra hours over the past few months to ensure that the results of his unit stayed at the same level. Peter has been caught between expectations and results: $E \gg R$ (see Chapter 2). When queried it appeared that Peter set these expectations for himself: 'I think a good manager should be able to rely on himself, irrespective of the expectations of others.' In itself, that is a good way to think. However, further inquiry revealed that Peter is afraid of being rejected if he asks for help. His ego, the Independent One, has taken over. When asked about the reason for his apprehension, he said that he had come across several cases in another company where people who had asked for help were frowned upon by colleagues. He decided that this was not going to happen to him. This shows that, deep down, he is afraid to be labelled in a certain way by others.

The moral of this story is that it does not immediately have to be apparent that you are behaving the way you do because you want to be labelled in a certain way by others. It usually turns out that your behaviour is driven strictly by an intrinsic 'want to', as opposed to an extrinsic 'have to'.

Incidentally, the link with internal and external norms is quite apparent here: external norms (which you have stored in your inner world) are more likely to trigger the use of an ego than internal norms.

Alternating egos

What also makes it difficult to recognise egos is that they can alternate in a flash. Your environment could very easily change after you started to use the Nice One. This could prompt you to bring out the Demolisher, since every perceived change in your environment sets off its own association and evaluation process. To complicate matters, you can also use a combination of egos. Can you imagine what the combination of the Demolisher and the Sweet Talker would look like? This combination takes you down with a smile. Or the combination of the Adviser and the Powerful One: you give someone advice but if she doesn't follow it things will end badly for her. It is not practical to list all the possible combinations here. What's most important is that you realise that the eight egos form the basis for the positioning issues that have been discussed and that any combination is possible. I invite you to submit your own examples of other ego combinations to the website.

Rule of thumb

How do you quickly recognise when an ego comes into play? Ask yourself what the intention of your behaviour towards others is. Your ego takes over:

1. When you intend to position yourself in relation to others.

2. When the main intention of your behaviour is to be labelled in a certain way.

When should egos be overruled?

You should only overrule your ego if it is having an adverse effect on you, or if you think it will start to have an adverse effect on you. Egos are initially very helpful in achieving certain results. In my descriptions of the eight egos, I emphasised negative aspects for the negative self-fulfilling prophecies, as people usually run into blocks they don't understand themselves. Now you know that you have egos and that you can overrule them, if you choose to do so. It is important not to deal with your egos until the negative self-fulfilling prophecy resulting from their use starts to have an adverse effect on you. Also, when using them, examine your egos in greater detail if you feel your good qualities are about to disappear from view.

Once again, it is quite difficult to recognise the barriers raised by egos since the behaviour often appears to be so natural. Experience has taught us that over time people increasingly feel the need for self-reflection. They increase their effectiveness by gaining greater insight into themselves and the reasons for displaying certain behaviour. They reach a time in life when they start to ask themselves existential questions, such as: 'Who am I really?', 'Why am I here?', 'What's the meaning of all this?', 'Why am I not really satisfied, even though I've got everything my heart desires?'

Some readers will recognise this, others may not. Some readers will not recognise anything of the themes discussed above. 'Egos? Fortunately, they don't bother me!' Fine, we can only respect such an assertion. They have, as it were, not yet been adversely affected by these deep-seated patterns, or they (still) don't feel the need to dig deeper. For these readers, the most they can take away from this is to understand others better. This will enable them to help others who run into ego blocks, or to provide others with insights that will enable them to develop further.

PROJECTING PROBLEMS ONTO THE EGO LAYER

If you can't solve a problem on the norms layer, and you think that this has to do with the negative aspects of your ego, it is important to redefine the problem. So far the problems have been defined as:

- My environment is the problem (environmental layer).

- What should I do to solve my problem with my environment? What should I do to feel happy again? (behavioural layer).

- How can I influence my environment (*to feel happy again*)? (skills layer).

- Which stimulating or restrictive norm should *take precedence in order for me to solve* my problem with my environment? (norms layer).

The problem on the ego layer is then redefined as:

Which egos should I let go of or use to solve my problem with my environment (so that I can feel happy again)?

There are two stages to the model:

1. First determine which egos might be getting in your way.

2. Then try to find out how you can overrule these egos authentically using your values, or accept the fact that you use these egos.

You often use your ego when you think your environment is unsafe, or when you are afraid of how your environment might react. You are afraid of a certain consequence. By using your ego, you hedge your bets. You influence your environment by displaying ego behaviour. Because of your past experiences, you know (subconsciously) that your environment will react in a certain way to your ego. You display ego behaviour to elicit a certain response from others. Once again, your fear motive, not your creation motive, usually leads the way here. Unfortunately, your ego limits your successes to the short-term. Your credibility and happiness might crumble away in the long-term. It is sometimes difficult to recognise and acknowledge your egos in certain situations. It is not always behaviour you can be proud of. However, by taking a good look at yourself, you will make it possible to develop your authenticity. On the other hand, we have seen that your egos can benefit you. When you use them, make sure you do so consciously.

You can make a conscious choice about whether you want to transcend your ego or you could choose to use a specific ego. First decide which ego might be getting in your way and what your intention is. Try to establish what move in position you are making in relation to the other person. Determine how you would like to be labelled by the other person (rule of thumb). Listen carefully to your inner voice, your self-talk. This voice tells you why you should or should not do something. This voice expresses the fear you feel at that particular point in time for a specific ego. For example, the Nice One may say: 'Be careful, or you'll be excluded from the group. They must like you.' The Powerful One: 'Be careful, if you don't speak up strongly now, your authority will be undermined.' Self-talk often gives you the advice to use a certain type of ego. Appendix 2 contains examples of negative and positive self-talk for each of the eight egos. Positive self-talk is a better path to your authenticity (see Chapter 7) and will help you to create a positive self-fulfilling prophecy. If you recognise the ego you call into play, you will immediately know that you are trying to make a certain move. You also know that you run a certain risk when you let your ego get the better of you, such as a negative self-fulfilling prophecy.

TRY THIS...

This assignment contains a description of how you can decide whether or not to overrule an ego. Look at how you worked through the other exercises in this chapter and work out the example below. The best thing you can do is to write down what you stand to gain from using your ego, the reward you will receive, the risks you avoid.

You realise...

You prevent...
Unfortunately, as discussed, using your ego comes at a price. List all the costs.

It will cost me...

I risk...

Use this analysis to decide if you want your ego to lead the way or if you want to investigate further how you would behave if you were to put your values (Chapter 6) or your mission (Chapter 7) in the forefront. Once again, you can make a conscious choice to let your ego be in control. You stand to gain a lot from this in the short-term. In any case, you will make a conscious choice. If you have recognised your ego and want to find out how you can resolve the situation authentically, it is important to proceed to the next layer (the norms layer), since your values will enable you to overrule your egos.

SUMMARY

Your inner world contains several egos which underlie some of your behaviour. An ego aims to position itself in a certain way in relation to others: above or alongside another person. An ego wants to secure your position in the group. All egos have a powerful and an exaggerated variant.

Whereas the powerful variant can strengthen your authenticity and prevent you from losing your position in the group, the exaggerated variant will cause you to lose your position.

We can distinguish eight different egos:

- Ego 1: the Proud One, the Show-off

- Ego 2: the Independent One, the Soloist

- Ego 3: the Defender, the Victim

- Ego 4: the Quiet One, the Dodger

- Ego 5: the Nice One, the Sweet Talker

- Ego 6: the Relativist, the Envious One

- Ego 7: the Adviser, the Paternalist

- Ego 8: the Powerful One, the Demolisher

The deeper reward of an ego is to (still) make a difference or, negatively put, to prevent you from not making a difference and losing your position in the group. It is therefore an effective way to ensure recognition. An ego is called into play because you label your environment in a certain way, usually as unsafe. An unsafe environment is an environment in which you think you won't achieve the desired result by being yourself, or in which you think your position in the group is the subject of discussion. You must therefore be labelled in a certain way. You pull a successful trick and you secure your position. By doing so you make yourself dependent on others, since they, and not you, determine how you are labelled. They determine whether you make a difference, not you. Your egos are usually called into play without you being aware of it. They can benefit you in the short-term but if you call your ego into play for too long, a negative self-fulfilling prophecy could come into play; your fears will actually come true and you may lose your desired position in the group. You might not be aware of the use of your ego, but could just feel that something is keeping you from being happy, without knowing what it is.

You also saw that others can take advantage of your egos, and that to be labelled by yourself in a certain way is often a translation of how others label you. What is difficult about recognising an ego is that egos can alternate in a flash and that you can use a combination of egos. You shouldn't deal with an ego until it has, or you think it will have, an adverse effect on you, i.e. when the costs exceed the benefits. The exaggerated egos of one person trigger those of another. It is therefore good to know your exaggerated variants and allergies. We can identify a few natural allergies between egos.

Your ego can be called into play in three different ways: (1) based on the creation motive, in order to do things more easily your way; (2) based on the fear motive, in order to prevent loss of position; (3) from the exaggerated variant, which can result in a negative self-fulfilling prophecy.

The problem on the ego layer can be defined as 'Which egos should I let go of or use to solve my problem with my environment (so that I can feel happy again)?' Your values and mission can help you here.

The core of Authentic Leadership is to recognise your egos and use them consciously (or not at all).

6
The values layer

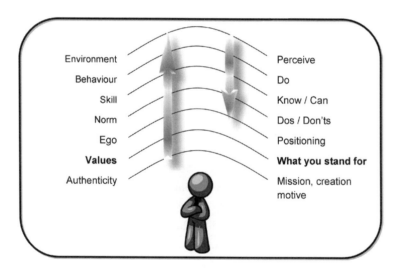

Environment	Perceive
Behaviour	Do
Skill	Know / Can
Norm	Dos / Don'ts
Ego	Positioning
Values	**What you stand for**
Authenticity	Mission, creation motive

The values layer is situated two layers below the norms layer, and although different, norms and values are intrinsically connected. In this chapter I discuss how norms relate to values. Cultural differences (within companies) arise from different norms and values. I cover different ways of dealing with cultural differences and cultural development. I then address the problems associated with this layer and the values that represent your authenticity.

When we talk about values, we talk about beliefs, dogmas, fundamental principles, deeper convictions. Values have a higher level of abstraction than norms (when you talk about norms, you're talking about rules of conduct). The word 'value' can be used to mean *a fundamental principle you stand for*. This concerns such things as respect, integrity, independence, honesty, etc. (Appendix 1 contains a list of common values). Without being aware of it, you often behave according to your values. Authentic leaders are highly aware of these values. Because your core values say much about your authentic self, it is important to examine them carefully.

TRY THIS...

Which three values would you most like to govern your decisions? Take your time to think about this. It may help to imagine that you are responsible for raising a child you love dearly. Which three core values would you like to pass on to this child? Try to describe them in order of importance.

It is certainly possible that, after a while, you might reach a deeper understanding and want to give precedence to other values. You may come to realise that there are more than three values that are important in your life. However, the idea is to imprint these three values so firmly in your inner world that you apply them automatically whenever you're faced with important decisions. These three values will help you to make quick, authentic decisions in complex and urgent situations. I use the word 'authentic' because these values say much about your deepest self. They form an important part of the personal mission statement you will define in Chapter 7.

HOW DO NORMS AND VALUES RELATE TO EACH OTHER?

Values are the fundamental principles on which internal norms are based. The norms and values of a particular environment combine to form its *culture*. Every environment has its own culture. Even in the smallest of groups, consisting of two people, 'rules of conduct' are established. These (usually unwritten) norms and values are formed when people spend time with each other. All newly formed groups go through a phase in which the *dos and don'ts* of living together are (subconsciously) defined. In this way, groups, communities, businesses, countries or religions develop a consistent set of norms and values which they regard as the foundation for their way of coexisting.

Your values and mission form the basis of your authentic behaviour (see Chapter 7). Your internal norms are the rules of conduct that stem from your values. Your values and internal norms combine to form your authentic culture. A conflict may arise on the norms layer between internal and external norms (imposed by your environment). Authentic Leadership means you have thought so carefully about your values and their corresponding norms that your internal norms always take precedence over external ones. Thinking carefully about your values and their corresponding norms will also help you at the outer limit of your comfort zone. We already saw that your personal growth is stunted (without you being aware of it) at the outer limit of your comfort zone by your hidden restrictive norms (see Chapter 4). Your well-considered internal norms will now become your stimulating norms, thereby helping you to move from your comfort zone into your growth zone.

Incidentally, you could allow values other than your three core values to become paramount in different environments. For instance, a company may choose to emphasise the values that will best support its strategy over the next three years. A company's core values are often expressed in its mission statement. Company values usually don't conflict with the values of individual employees, but rather complement them. If you do encounter such a conflict, you might want to ask yourself if you really want to commit to that company. You are more likely to come across conflicts on the norms layer. A few examples of values and their corresponding norms are given in Appendix 1.

There is usually a notable culture change in companies after a change in management. New managers introduce their own norms and values. They will – both consciously and subconsciously – encourage behaviour which, in their perception, is appropriate and discourage behaviour they consider inappropriate. Because a manager has authority, she will be able to exercise influence on the organisation's dos and don'ts. When new staff members are recruited, she will (subconsciously) favour those who observe the same norms and values as herself. A company usually starts to adopt the culture of its leader after about two years. If a company culture is very homogeneous, it may not tolerate the new director's culture. In that case, the director will not have created enough support and must step down.

CULTURAL DIFFERENCES

I have observed something amazing in my work with people from different cultural backgrounds: it appears that norms, not values, lie at the heart of cultural clashes. A simple example is the value of 'respect'. For example, if you want to do business with people from another culture you will show them respect. This also holds true for potential partners within your own culture, so this shouldn't be a problem. Although respect is an important value in both situations, things get really interesting on the norms layer when the rules that stem from this value clash. For example, in Arabic cultures, it is considered rude for the sole of your foot or shoe to be visible. So crossing your legs in a meeting in a way that reveals the sole of your shoe could mean that discussions are quickly brought to an end. Even though you have tried to show respect, a conflict will arise as a result of a norm. There are cultures where it is respectful to speak your mind, while this is considered extremely disrespectful in other cultures. These are situations where the values are the same but the norms are different. You also come across this phenomenon in organisational cultures. All environments translate values into norms in different ways.

The reason cultures rarely clash over values is that values are more abstract and thus less defined than norms. Because norms consist of rules of conduct and (generally accepted) standards, conflicts are largely felt on this layer. A person either obeys or disobeys a rule. This can easily be measured. If a norm is violated, we believe that person doesn't respect our values. This is not necessarily true. At most, the other person may be observing a different norm, rather than a different value. In the case of norm conflicts, people tend to focus on the differences. Because of selective perception, they only become more convinced of the 'wrongness' of the other culture. Because people also have a tendency to impose their norms on others, things can quickly escalate. A good example of the negative self-fulfilling prophecy is: this collaboration can't possibly succeed. What makes things difficult is that people usually react from their egos when 'their' values are being challenged, with all the concomitant risks, since this feels as if their deeper selves are being attacked. The values that underlie these norms are rarely questioned in a conflict, since both parties could very well hold the same values. So, a conflict could be resolved 'from the inside out', i.e. a solution is not imposed 'from the outside'. Some norms can continue to exist side by side, as long as they stem from the same value. In this way, you not only accept a person as she is, but also *her norm*. It is the only way to realise (measurable) cultural development within a short space of time (e.g. after a merger).

The fact that conflicts are often fought out over values, while they are actually norm conflicts, is quite an eye-opener for many people. It makes the conflicts less of an issue. It is very effective to resolve conflicts on the basis of shared values. This applies to most cultural problems in business, in regional and even religious contexts. Imagine if everyone could understand this. It would enable us to define shared norms that can exist side by side based on shared values, and not just based on historically imposed norms. This could help resolve many conflicts in the world.

TRY THIS...

What intercultural conflicts do you come across in your environment, for example in your street, family, company or in your country? Try to work out whether these are norm or value conflicts.

CULTURAL DEVELOPMENT

It is now very common to orient towards culture in companies (e.g. after mergers and acquisitions, or following a major change of strategy). If everyone agrees on the values and their corresponding norms, less guidance will be needed since people will agree about certain things. This will increase efficiency and necessitate fewer adjustments. A company will thereby become self-cleansing. People who no longer fit in with the company will eventually leave. People who do fit in will stay or will join the company.

However, experience has taught me that many cultural development programmes are enthusiastically launched but then quickly fizzle out. Many directors aren't aware of the *pitfalls* of these programmes. You see the same thing happening on a smaller scale during what are referred to as 'team-building sessions'. I will summarise the main pitfalls below:

Model behaviour A company's cultural development programme can only succeed if it is in keeping with the norms and values of the directors. The solution: choose core values that are in keeping with the strategy and that are highly prized by the directors so that they will model the desired behaviour. If there is a clash between company and personal values directors will not model the desired behaviour, and a lack of good modelling is deadly for any cultural development process. People look for reasons (without being aware of it) for not having to step out of their comfort zone. Poor model behaviour is the best justification for not having to change yourself. Don't automatically roll out the programme to the next organisational level until that level recognises model behaviour at the higher level. If the next level still doesn't recognise this behaviour, the higher organisational level will have to work on this further.

Staff involvement Cultural development programmes won't succeed if staff members haven't had any say in defining the desired culture. They will feel like management playthings. At least take stock of the wishes of these culture carriers and involve them in the creation of the new culture. You may be surprised to find that staff members actually embrace the same values as the directors.

Concrete and measurable Cultural development programmes cannot succeed until new values are translated into norms. Only when you start to make values 'measurable' by linking them to stimulating norms will things become concrete enough for you to be able to act on and to control. It is also essential to uncover an organisation's restrictive norms. This could be one of the main reasons for cultural development programmes failing. Programmes get off to a good start; stimulating norms are identified and listed. But then staff members seem to fall back into their old behaviour. This doesn't mean that nothing was learned; as the organisation starts to expand, its comfort zone will expand at some point and form a new outer limit. And you know what happens at the outer limit: restrictive norms take over and try to bring you back to safety. If you're not aware of the restrictive norms present in the organisation, this will surprise and frustrate you: why are they not changing? Now is the time to prove how strong the organisation is. In a cultural development programme, you should already be aware of the restrictive norms since they are bound to crop up again. In fact, as we saw in chapter 4, restrictive norms don't go away; they just slip into the background until they are needed again. Accept this and decide how restrictive norms should be dealt with. A step-by-step plan will be very useful here. If you see restrictive norm behaviour in your organisation, discuss it immediately and decide whether this just happened or whether it was deliberate. Don't get angry or give up, but accept it when you launch a cultural development programme. It's not a problem, it's manageable. Everyone has good reasons for behaving the way they do. The trick is to find out together what the restrictive norms achieve. This will enable you to anticipate and intervene more quickly in future clashes at the outer limit of the comfort zone since these clashes are never-ending. The exact same restrictive and stimulating norms will clash, which is good since it shows that an organisation is expanding, or needs to take action if the environment isn't secure.

Ownership A cultural development programme will not be supported if staff members haven't been able to commit themselves personally at some point to the new norms and values (see the management cycle in Chapter 3). By checking ownership, you will increase the personal responsibility of every staff member to contribute to the creation of the desired culture. Here 'ownership' means that staff members agree with the desired norms and values, want to propagate them, want to be held accountable for them and want to hold others accountable for them to help them implement the desired culture. Hold regular feedforward sessions in the first year. Cultural development will become embedded by allowing staff members to gain firsthand experience of the usefulness of investing in each other.

In Appendix 4 I sum up the results of our investigation into twelve success and failure factors in a cultural development programme. In Appendix 5 I analyse how you can tackle a successful programme.

PROJECTING PROBLEMS ONTO THE VALUES LAYER

If you can't work things out on the norms or ego layer and want to delve further to solve your problem, it is vital to examine the problem. So far the problems have been defined as:

- My environment is the problem (environmental layer).

- What should I do to solve my problem with my environment? What should I do to feel happy again? (behavioural layer).

- How can I influence my environment (in order to feel happy again)? (skills layer).

- Which stimulating or restrictive norm should take precedence in order for me to solve my problem with my environment? (norms layer).

- Which egos should I let go of or use in order to be able to properly solve my problem with my environment (so that I can feel happy again)? (ego layer).

The problem on the values layer can be defined as follows:

How should I behave towards my environment if I let myself be guided by my values (so that I will feel happy again)?

Earlier, you chose three values which you stand for. By asking yourself about these values, other association and evaluation processes take place in your inner world. As a result, you gain insight into how you would behave if you were honest with yourself. By acting according to these values, a few internal stimulating norms will immediately come to the fore which will enable you to measure your behaviour. For example, imagine 'honesty' is your core value. In the example of the controlling boss you ask yourself 'How would I behave towards my boss if honesty was a driving factor?' You can probably imagine here that you would want to have an honest talk with your boss (value). You will then let your internal norms take the lead and make sure the talk focuses on solving problems (norm). You will use the right skills, feedforward (skill) amongst others, and subsequently be on your best behaviour (behaviour) with your boss (environment).

This analysis is also very effective at the outer limit of your comfort zone. It helps you overrule your restrictive norms. You will thus see a move from the deeper layers towards the outermost layer – unlike a move where the environment is the determining factor (since the external norm will determine your behaviour and the skills to be used). You can therefore change direction from the 'outside inwards' to the 'centre outwards'. *Authentic behaviour always moves from the centre outwards. If you succeed in this, it will give you the deepest sense of fulfilment.*

If, after weighing up the consequences, you decide not to deal with things, you will know that your restrictive norm has won out over your stimulating norm and that you can always fall back on complaining, lower your expectations, or leave.

TRY THIS...

You can go deeper than this by combining the results of a number of exercises. Go over the results of the exercise in Chapter 2 in which you described the environments you want to invest in. Which three values do you want to apply the most in each environment? Come up with at least two internal norms for each value.

SUMMARY

Values are more deeply rooted than norms. A value can be defined as a fundamental principle you stand for. It forms the basis for your internal norms. The combination of norms and values in a particular environment is referred to as its 'culture'. Every environment has its own culture. It appears that norms, not values, lie at the heart of cultural clashes. It is therefore good to clearly distinguish between norms and values. You can solve many problems by first reaching consensus about the values and then jointly defining the norms.

The success or failure of cultural development programmes depends on the model behaviour of the management, involving staff members at an early stage and demanding ownership, translating the values into restrictive and stimulating norms and making cultural development measurable.

The problem on the values layer is defined as 'How should I behave towards my environment if I am led by my values (so that I can feel happy again)?'

You are well advised to think about this carefully in advance. It is a necessity for Authentic Leadership. It enables you to live from the centre outwards. Authentic behaviour always moves from the centre outwards. The problem on the values layer will help you find the stimulating norms you need to move from the comfort zone to the growth zone.

7
The authenticity layer

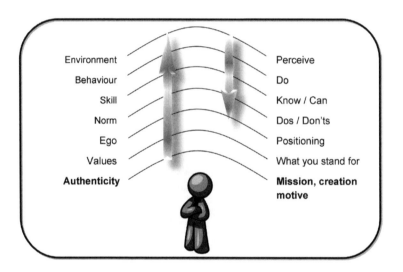

Environment		Perceive
Behaviour		Do
Skill		Know / Can
Norm		Dos / Don'ts
Ego		Positioning
Values		What you stand for
Authenticity		**Mission, creation motive**

The authenticity layer lies below the values layer. Authentic Leadership is founded on this layer. It is the most important layer, the one which gives life meaning. A number of fundamental questions will be dealt with in this chapter, such as: What really makes me happy? What achievements would I like to make? How can I manage to operate more independently in my environment from within my 'self'? What would I like to contribute to the world around me? Why does authentic behaviour give me the best chance to achieve happiness and results?

Imagine. It's Christmas Day. You have taken the trouble to buy a present for a child you love very much. This child still believes in Santa Claus. You had lots of fun looking for the right present. You secretly add yours to the pile of presents. As you do so, you see a present which has your name on it. Interesting. The time has come. You can open your own present. It turns out to be a nice one. Good. The child is then given your present. The child opens it excitedly. When she sees what it is she begins to glow with happiness. She gets up and shouts: 'Thank you Santa Claus!'

What makes you happier? Opening your own present or watching the child unwrap hers? Probably the latter. Who gets the credit? Santa Claus! Isn't it amazing? Why does this make you feel so happy? It's a simple example, but captures the essence of Authentic Leadership. The ingredients are: positive intention, giving unconditionally, seeing someone else develop further, happiness, not necessarily wanting to be labelled in a certain way or positioning yourself.

The concept of authenticity is examined in greater detail in this chapter. I discuss the concepts of mission and vision within the context of authenticity, the pros and cons of authenticity, the workings of authenticity in your inner world, the ability to give and receive, giving and forgiving, the problem on the authenticity layer, and finally, a few tips on recognising authentic behaviour.

WHAT IS AUTHENTICITY?

Below I reiterate a few statements on authenticity which have been dealt with in this book:

- The core of Authentic Leadership is to let the creation motive drive your behaviour.

- Authentic Leadership is the ability to turn fear motives into creation motives.

- Authentic Leadership is the ability to lead yourself and others according to the creation motive. The creation, in combination with a sense of fulfilment, is your reward.

- Your values form the basis for authentic behaviour.

- Authentic leaders are highly aware of these values.

- Your values and internal norms combine to form your authentic culture.

- Authentic Leadership means that you have thought so carefully about your values and their corresponding norms that these internal norms always take the lead.

- Authentic behaviour always moves from the centre outwards.

A few terms:

- 'Authenticity' means genuineness and, therefore, reliability.

- Authentic Leadership amounts to 'exerting influence with your mission in mind, in a genuine and reliable way'.

- Authentic behaviour is behaviour that arises from your true self rather than from your ego. Your ego is sometimes a façade. It is often a trick. By contrast, authentic behaviour is real. You behave in this way because this is who you are. You don't want to be labelled in any way, or to position yourself, since you already know who you are and what you stand for.

- Your deepest motive, on which your behaviour is based, lies hidden within your authenticity. This deepest motive is your mission. Your mission is what gives your life meaning, what you are going to contribute to the world.

- A vision is an image of a desired future.

- Many people understand 'leadership' to mean 'managing others'. However, within the context of this book, I use the term 'leadership' in the sense of 'being an influencer'.

- Authentic Leadership is a form of personal leadership. Personal leadership concerns leadership of yourself, enabling you to lead others more effectively. Authentic Leadership concerns leadership of yourself *and* others and comes from your mission.

- The authenticity layer is the deepest layer of your existence, your core. It is the source from which everything emanates.

AUTHENTICITY: GIVING BASED ON YOUR MISSION

Imagine that you were put on earth with a mission, although you don't know what it is. Throughout your life you are rewarded by the world at large whenever you behave in a way that is in keeping with your mission. Your reward is a nice feeling. Would you eventually work out what your mission is? That would be nice, since once you have discovered your mission, you'll be able to consciously choose to behave as much as possible according to your mission and thus feel happy as often as possible.

Authentic leaders know what their mission is. They have already discovered it. It doesn't matter if they were born with a mission or if they created one. They have a mission and live accordingly. In every decision they make, they are able to refer back to this mission. It is their guide. You also have a mission. Perhaps you've already discovered it, or perhaps you are still searching for it.

A mission and a vision

These two words are often used interchangeably. In Chapter 2 I defined a vision as: *an image of a desired future*. This is not the same as a mission. *A mission expresses your sense of purpose, what you continually want to contribute to your environment and yourself.* A mission is not a future goal, but something you do on a daily basis. For example:

- A teacher's mission is to teach others.

- A soldier's mission is to defend his country.

- A fireman's mission is to put out fires.

- The fireman is also a father. As a father, his mission is to raise his children.

- The mission of most people is to elevate themselves and others to a higher level.

The above examples show that you can have different roles and therefore different missions in your 'being'. The main feature of a mission is that you contribute or create something. You create things by the very fact that you exist. Even when you're not doing anything, you're creating carbon dioxide, heat, sweat, energy. In fact, it's impossible not to create. You exist, therefore you create. Your mission is determined exclusively by the specific form of your creation. The challenge is to discover or devise this mission.

The question of how one comes by a mission can be answered in several different ways. Some people feel that a higher power has given them a mission. Others discover their mission by looking back and realising that they have been creating something specific all their life. There are those who recognise a mission because they experience a sense of fulfilment when they do certain kinds of work. And then there are those who make something their mission at some point because they think it's important for the future. What's most important is that you choose your own mission and you decide what you want to contribute to the world around you. It doesn't really matter how you come by your mission, as long as you know or decide what your missions are at some point, since this will enable you to focus your behaviour on them. You will thus become more effective and experience a greater sense of fulfilment. Just producing carbon dioxide will not really give you a sense of fulfilment. A characteristic of a good mission is that the more you grasp the added value of your mission, the greater your sense of fulfilment. After all, the more you feel that you 'make a difference', the greater your sense of fulfilment. A mission is what you want to create, not what you have to create. It's your choice, your happiness.

Missions usually focus on other people but a note is called for here. Some people choose a mission which doesn't focus on their own kind, the human species. Some people choose a mission which focuses on other species, objects or art forms. Incidentally, humans often still feature prominently in the background of these missions. An example is 'It's my life's mission to create works of art that move people' or 'It's my mission to convince others that they shouldn't kill whales'. In this book, I only discuss missions that are focused on other people.

It will give you a sense of fulfilment if – as part your mission, without selling yourself short – you elevate the people around you to a higher level (this sense of fulfilment was discussed in Chapter 2). Seeing your final creation proves that you exist, that you make a difference. It brings recognition. Much more important than a 'theory' is what you see in practice: people who elevate something to a higher level according to their (sometimes subconscious) mission experience a greater sense of fulfilment. They feel proud and valued. The nice thing is that you inspire loyalty in others. They start to feel you are seriously trying to create something, in them and in their environment. They recognise – and can identify with – your mission. They may even feel that they have the same mission. People who help themselves *and* others to develop further will not only experience a greater sense of fulfilment, they will also achieve better results than people who only improve themselves. Achieving the best results comes from the fact that by acting according to your authenticity, you always give the best you've got. Time and time again. It is therefore logical to assume that you will eventually achieve the best possible results.

Positive intention

In summary, you could say that the authentic behaviour which arises from your mission contributes something to your environment so that this environment can be elevated to a higher level. You could call this 'giving with a positive intention' or 'creating according to your mission' (see Figure 7.1).

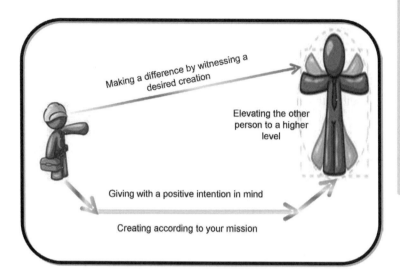

Figure 7.1 Giving with a positive intention or creating according to your mission

A few aspects of Figure 7.1 can be found in the Christmas Day example. You did your best to find the nicest present (the best results) to make the child happy. Looking for this present was rewarding in itself. Why did it make you feel good when you saw that the child was so happy? Not because she thanked you, since the man with the red hat and white beard received the credit and the thanks. It was therefore not your ego, since nobody knew the present came from you. It was authentic, it was genuine, not a trick. You were probably so happy because you witnessed a creation which you had brought to fruition. You were able to give this child something, to make her happy. You gave with a positive intention. Through the change in the child you recognised that you 'make a difference'. You made this possible because you are who you are.

Our organisation has asked thousands of leaders from around the world what really makes them happy. The same examples of seeing development in their environment kept cropping up – development which they helped facilitate. It made these leaders even happier than 'scoring because of their ego'.

In short, life is a gift and it is up to you to give it meaning. Your most authentic mission is to give the best of yourself. This is why it is important to find out why, with what mission, or for what purpose you were put on this earth.

TRY THIS...

It can be a challenge to put your mission(s) into words. The software on the website http://www.authentiekleiderschap.nl/en/discovermission can help you define your mission. You will also find examples of missions on the website (you can of course try this mission on paper).

You have already described the environments you want to invest in and developed a vision for each environment. This gave you a sense of direction. You will now define a mission for each environment, so first choose an environment.

1. Target group: What target group(s) would you like to invest in? (Example: leaders.)

2. Describe when you felt happy with this or a similar target group; choose examples where you saw the target group develop. (Example: when insight into their authentic mission and powerful egos boosts their self-confidence.)

3. Creation: What creation of the target group made you happy? (Example: developing Authentic Leadership.)

4. Giving: What was the nicest/best thing you gave them of yourself, to enable the creation to come to fruition? (Example: insight into their mission and powerful egos.)

This is the most difficult and fascinating exercise in this book, since it is very important to formulate it correctly. Don't be modest when answering these questions. Share your best qualities. I would prefer you to get someone (a trusted friend, a colleague, a coach) to help you with this assignment. Or you could use our website to find a sparring partner who can help you.

It may help you define your mission if you write down your answers in order:

Mission: I give (answer 1) (answer 4) so that (answer 1) (answer 3).
Example: I give (leaders) (insight ino their mission and powerful egos) so that (leaders) (develop Authentic Leadership)

To help you answer question 4, you can follow these steps:

a. Look at your working environment. First write down an example of a time when you had a lot of fun and success with others, when you felt thrilled and energised. Replay this scene in your mind. Who else was involved? What results did you achieve? What was the atmosphere like?

b. Now write down what you contributed to this team or that person. Look for as many things as possible. For example: you gave others space, you provided clarity, you provided alternatives, you allowed others to engage in self-reflection, you gave them assignments, you broke down their barriers. Write them all down.

c. When you go over the list, try to identify the common thread in the things you create: what do you contribute to your environment so that it can grow? What is your best and most typical characteristic which enables others to develop in your environment? Try to select three main points (ones which are easy to remember so you can use them later).

You have now defined your mission in this environment. You can fill in questions 1–4 for every environment you want to invest in. Try to define your mission as concisely as possible (the more succinct, the better).

Example 1: 'I provide my team with security, insight into their barriers and the tools to overcome them so that they can achieve their objectives more successfully and with a greater sense of ful-filment.'

What is interesting is that answer 3 of this exercise is actually the shortest description of your mission, what it is you want to create, your 'slogan'. You can imprint this slogan into your inner world. It may help you at the outer limit of your comfort zone to find out what you need to do if you want your mission to drive your behaviour. Simply ask yourself 'What would I do now if my "slogan" was the determining factor?' For example, 'What would I do now if I helped people to lead with a greater sense of fulfilment and success.'

A few tips that may be helpful in your definition:

- Try to write a one-line sentence.

- Put the sentence in the first person singular and in the present tense ('I give' instead of 'I can/will give').

- List your achievements, not your abilities ('I gave' instead of 'I am able to give').

- Put things positively: describe the things you want to give.

- Don't compare yourself with others.

- Be realistic: you should be able to picture yourself doing it.

When you ask yourself these questions you are really looking for a mission that is already there without you being aware of it. You may of course want to decide on a future mission. In that case, decide on what you would most like to give your environment and make this your mission.

It may also help if you examine your natural interests during this 'soul searching'. What really moves you? What kind of books do you read? What kind of television programmes do you find inter-esting? Who inspires you? You can use all these sources of informa-tion for your mission. Now try to find out why that is so for each of these questions. What does this say about your deeper motives?

The link to values

A mission statement also expresses the values you would like to see take precedence in the things you do. It denotes how you carry out your mission. You have previously defined the values you would like to see take precedence in a particular environment. Write these values down under the specific mission you defined. Your mission statement is now complete.

Example 1: 'I provide my team with security, insight into their barriers and the tools to overcome them so that they can achieve their objectives with a greater sense of fulfilment and success. My dominant values here are: integrity, responsibility and freedom of thought.'

Example 2: 'I help people to feel more fulfilled and to be more successful. I stand for integrity, assuming responsibility and freedom of thought.'

A vision for a mission

This is where you describe what the future will be like if you allow your mission to drive your behaviour for a few years. Fill in: If I have given (answer 1) (answer 4) for a few years so (answer 1) (answer 3), my vision can be expressed as…

For example: If I have given leaders some understanding of their missions and powerful egos for a few years so they were able to develop their Authentic Leadership, my vision can be expressed as follows: an organisation with leaders who give the best they've got in order to bring out the best in others, so that happiness and success go hand in hand.

It also holds true here that you can use your mission to define a vision for any particular environment.

The mission

You have now prepared specific mission statements for several specific environments. A career or work related mission will be different from a family mission. Now try to define *the* mission, a mission that expresses the core of your being. You can do this by going over questions 1–4 again and filling in 'my environment' for answer 1. You can use the values you defined in Chapter 6.

The vision

Taking *the* mission as a starting-point, you can define *the* vision. For example: My vision is a world (environment) where people use their mission to give the best they've got to others and others do likewise for them so that everyone feels more fulfilled and is more successful.

This definition shows that, although a vision can go beyond what you go through in this life, it will nevertheless continue to serve as a guide for your daily activities. You are advised to make a step-by-step plan for how you can realise your vision from the here and now. This will enable you to be focused in your activities. Try to decide what you will do differently tomorrow, next week, in a month's time, perhaps next year. Put your shoulder into it. Have a look in your diary and decide how you can prepare for meetings using your mission. You will see that you can put things in a certain order: you have a mission, you create a vision, you make a step-by-step plan, you focus on the here and now. Every step brings you closer to your vision and reflects your mission.

You should realise that a mission does not have to be something static. You grow, you develop. If, at some point, you see that this new mission is even better, you might choose to expand or revise your mission. I often find that leaders are more likely to rediscover their mission than to discover something entirely new, since all the ingredients are already there in your inner world. I sincerely hope that, once you have (re)discovered your mission, you will (re)discover what a beautiful person you are, that you can rightly be proud of your deepest motives, that you will start to live according to these motives again.

Now that you have defined your mission, it will be possible to lead yourself and others according to it. You are now able to make yourself and your environment more effective, more successful and happier through Authentic Leadership.

You can find other missions and visions on the website (www.authentiekleiderschap.nl/en). They may inspire you to define your own mission and vision. I invite you to share these with others on the website, so that you give them the opportunity to define their own missions and visions more effectively.

TRY THIS...

- Make a step-by-step plan for one or more visions.

- Next week, determine which mission you would like to see take precedence in the decisions you make. Also examine which positive self-fulfilling prophecy you might set in motion.

- Help a few people whom you want to invest in to define their mission and vision.

A mission for a team or organisation

My experience is that the mission statements of organisations and teams are often impersonal. They are well-phrased sentences intended to impress stakeholders but which rarely express what makes staff members proud or happy. The best mission is one you heard a staff member come out with spontaneously at a party. It expresses the growth your organisation wants to see happen with your client. It indicates your sense of purpose within the wider context of your organisation. Don't make it a complicated text, but try to express the mission in the simplest possible terms so that everyone can remember it.

Once again, what mission would you like a staff member to come out with? Why is she so happy to work for the company? What does she contribute to the client that makes her proud? Instead of a sales pitch selling a product or service, tell the client what gives you, the supplier, a sense of fulfilment: to see the client develop in a certain way.

If a staff member really lives a mission, she will be able to communicate this authentically. It stands to reason that a product or service needs to be paid for. Creating something for a client is worthwhile and she will be happy to pay for it. However, this is not the main objective.

You can answer the exercises you have undertaken throughout this book with your team or organisation. You may regard a team or organisation as a living being. What is your team mission? Try to describe the ideal staff member. What is her mission? Which three core values are important in staff collaboration and in collaboration with clients? Which egos are helpful, which ones are not? Which restrictive and stimulating norms arise in your team? What skills does the team require to behave appropriately towards the target group in their environment? You can fill in the seven layers and in doing so create a clear picture of the organisation as a whole.

For example, let's ask the four mission-related questions at organisation or team level so that we can define the mission of an organisation or team. In this case the organisation was a branch of the armed forces protecting diplomats in high risk areas:

1. Which target group? *The client.*

2. Describe happy moments (choose examples where you saw the client develop). For example, *becoming more successful or fulfilled by using the service or product.*

3. In what areas did they develop? *'Safety under extreme circumstances'.*

4. What was the nicest/best thing (about you) which you gave them so they could develop further? *Protection, insight and the ability to take action.*

Mission: Our organisation/team gives (answer 1) (answer 4) so that (answer 1) (answer 3).

> *Our organisation gives our clients protection, insight*
> *and the ability to take action so that they are safe under*
> *extreme circumstances.*

This can be refined to the slogan: *Creating safety under extreme circumstances.* The slogan gives focus and a sense of purpose. Staff members get the feeling that they really make a difference. This is precisely the reason why staff members are proud of their work.

ADVANTAGES AND DISADVANTAGES OF AUTHENTICITY

What's good about authenticity?

The main reason to opt for authenticity is that it gives you a greater sense of fulfilment. It gives you a real thrill when you see your creation develop. Some of the benefits you come across are the same as those for the creation motive:

- Authentic behaviour gives you the best chance to achieve success and experience a sense of fulfilment.

- Authentic behaviour motivates people to work towards a vision. It creates a pull factor. It gives you a thrill and works proactively. Authentic behaviour *generates* energy.

- While the vision for the future is clear, authentic behaviour focuses on the here and now. You are continually adding your value in the present moment. You give yourself completely to the activity. You enjoy using your skills on the path towards the objective and you feel connected with your environment. As a result, you will eventually achieve your highest goal with an intense sense of satisfaction.

- The reward of authentic behaviour is therefore twofold: on the one hand, the creation process is pleasurable since it makes you feel you are bringing out the best in yourself; on the other, it makes you feel good when another 'receives' your creation.

- Working according to a mission and vision also motivates the people around you. Many deep and rewarding relationships come from this. It mobilises forces to travel the same path. Holding on to a vision can bring out the best in others.

- It builds self-confidence. You feel that you make a difference and often see the evidence of this.

- Authentic behaviour is effective in the long-term.

- It is not a matter of 'having to' but of 'wanting to'. You are not a victim but an initiator: you are more likely to invite others than demand things from them.

- Authentic behaviour triggers authentic behaviour. When the people around you see that you really operate authentically, they will follow suit. In this way, you bring out the best in a duo, team, organisation, etc. Authentic behaviour inspires others. When you show your authenticity, you create a safe platform for others to display theirs. A good example is a successful team-building session. When the first member of a team really opens up by showing his authenticity, others are encouraged to follow suit. You will find that many people genuinely pursue a similar mission (perhaps we're all the same on the inside). The group thus develops a much deeper bond and commitment to jointly create something beautiful. People who receive something authentic from you will be only too happy to give you something authentic in return.

- Authentic behaviour brings about a positive self-fulfilling prophecy. If you feel that, thanks to your authenticity, you can experience your creation more often, your filter will open up to even more possibilities, even more opportunities. In every meeting or collaboration, you carefully look at how you can act according to your mission. Because you become a source of inspiration for others, they will give you even more opportunities to achieve your mission.

- Authentic behaviour makes you independent of the people around you. You don't require them to label you in a certain way in order to experience a sense of fulfilment. You demand nothing. After all, even if your gift is not received (which is of course a great pity), this doesn't alter the fact that you felt good during the creation process. You give unconditionally, and are therefore much more 'in control'.

- An added benefit is that you will start to receive – for no apparent reason – from unexpected parties. Many 'gifts' come your way when you are receptive to authentic giving and receiving. You will know by now that this partly has to do with your selective perception. As giving and receiving becomes an important story in your inner world relevant information will be allowed through your filters. Another reason why you will receive gifts is that you inspire people. This will be passed on to other colleagues and friends. People will want to be near you. Because you give the world a great deal of positivity, the world will also give you a great deal of positivity.

- Although this is not your goal, you may receive a lot of recognition. In authentic people, others subconsciously recognise something they would like to be themselves.

In fact, you can summarise the above as follows: authentic behaviour gives you the best chance to achieve success (achieving objectives for yourself and your environment) and happiness (the feeling you and the people around you have).

What are the risks of authentic behaviour?

Be careful not to become reckless. When you stop seeing the dangers and you give yourself completely to your mission, you could at some point take excessively large risks. It is good to move from your comfort zone to your growth zone where there are opportunities to achieve even more beautiful creations. However, if you venture too far from your comfort zone, you will end up in the reckless zone. You will then run the risk of meeting an unexpected disappointment since you didn't recognise the potential danger. 'Love is blind' is an appropriate saying here. The fear motive can help prevent you being reckless. So keep using your head.

It may happen that others don't receive the best you've got to give. You will then feel rejected. In the example of Christmas Day, this would mean that the child opens the present and disappointedly shouts 'I don't like this!' That hurts. Your present is not 'received'. Your disappointment is felt all the more because you had given the best you had. You should realise that you run this risk, since many people are not directly able to 'receive' your 'gift'. This is one of the main reasons people are afraid to be authentic: the fear of being hurt by others, since people feel vulnerable when they show their deepest self. Opening yourself up is generally referred to as 'showing your vulnerability'. If people were to take advantage of your openness it would really hurt. You would feel cut to the quick. This is why you choose to put on a layer we call 'ego' – it protects your vulnerability.

Another (temporary) risk you run with authentic behaviour is a lack of understanding in others. If you have really developed into someone who lets their positive intentions take the lead, who is in control of their egos, who lives according to a mission and pursues a vision giving precedence to values and internal norms, you will find that you start developing enormously, albeit with the usual ups and downs. You will become more independent, more self-aware, and will have a deeper understanding of the patterns that occur in yourself and in your environment. You will find it easier to give others feedforward (in the form of a compliment or a bit of advice). You will no longer be tempted to complain and gossip. The people around you will be able to tell that you are experiencing personal growth. Unfortunately, not everybody likes that. They may see your development as a threat. Although this wasn't your aim, you will move up in the group. Others may see this as a relative lowering of their own position. A few people might therefore bring out their egos to defend themselves against their perceived loss of position. This could even turn nasty in that they may try to stunt your development. You will see a kind of divide emerge: you have friends and colleagues who encourage you, and friends and colleagues who discourage you. Some people will be impressed by your development and might ask you to help them achieve a similar development. However, others will start to complain, to demolish, to dodge, to show-off … pick any ego. That hurts. I advise people who have been through this to see if they can accept it or decide whether they should confront others about it. However, if someone continues to try to stunt your development and you can't accept this and feel that you have done all you could, I would stop putting too much energy into it and either end the relationship or put it on the back burner.

HOW DOES AUTHENTICITY WORK?

If you have helped things develop using your mission hundreds of times, your filter will increasingly filter in other opportunities to accomplish your mission. You could say that you develop your authenticity as you encounter more positive examples. Your authentic self takes up an increasingly important position in your inner world. You will feel increasingly confident to show your deepest self. The positive self-fulfilling prophecy will then help you to contribute and create things in an increasing number of situations so that you will achieve better results and start to experience a greater sense of fulfilment. A description of how this works in your inner world is given below.

Selective perception This starts with selectively perceiving an event in your environment. You perceive events that have to do with your mission.

The association process You ask yourself where you have come across this before. Your inner world is then scanned in order to recognise such stories.

The evaluation process You ask yourself three questions:

1. *How should I label this information?* Is the information threatening or safe? You feel you can be yourself. You don't feel threatened in any way. You wonder how this situation can contribute to your mission.

2. *What potential consequences will this have?* What can you create or contribute? You see opportunities to elevate your environment to a higher level, to contribute something to your environment, to help it grow. Once again, this process will eventually take place without you being aware of it. The point is to first live through this process with greater awareness, until you feel that you become authentic increasingly naturally.

3. *What are the potential courses of action? What produces the greatest rewards?* Place all these different opportunities to help your environment

grow side-by-side and check which one has the highest reward. A vision will develop of what your environment will look like when you have been able to let it grow. You should also check which opportunity would give you the greatest sense of fulfilment, which creation you would consider the most beautiful. You will feel more and more connected with the world around you.

Behaviour Once you have selected the opportunities, use your skills to behave in such a way that your environment is elevated to a higher level. Although you know what you are working towards, your focus is wholly on the creation in the here and now. And you enjoy every move you make to realise your vision.

RECEIVING

Receiving from others

When you behave authentically towards another person you give her the means to enable her to develop in some way. This is your primary goal. You take satisfaction in trying, but it is all the more rewarding when the other person receives your 'gift'. This also applies when someone behaves authentically towards you. You should be able to receive. I will give a simple example. Someone says 'That's a nice suit!' To which you reply 'Oh, it was in the sale.' Sound familiar? Why do most people find it so difficult to receive a compliment? This has much to do with the recipient's ego:

1. The recipient doesn't completely trust the giver's sincerity. The giver could have ulterior motives (which is definitely the case with the Nice One).

2. This could mean that the recipient doesn't want to receive recognition (you will come across this with the Independent One, since recognition resembles help, which the Independent One doesn't want to receive).

3. It could be that the recipient feels compelled to return the favour, which is something she doesn't like doing.

4. The recipient may feel uncomfortable if he feels the compliment positions him above the rest of the group (which the Quiet One definitely wants to avoid, and will therefore do anything not to receive gifts).

So, there are various reasons why another person's gifts may not be received. My advice is to just accept. Thank the other person for the gift. Enjoy it. Do this both for yourself and for the other person. For yourself because you realise that you make a difference. You deserve it. And if it turns out that the other person has ulterior motives, act accordingly. Do it for the other person, because you are 'giving' him the chance to let his 'gift' be received. The moral of the story: the ability to receive gives others the opportunity to have their creations accepted (see Figure 7.2). It is good for you and for the other person. It is also interesting to point out that a compliment often registers, but that the recipient feels awkward at the moment of receipt. So don't be disconcerted by reserved behaviour if others don't immediately receive your compliment.

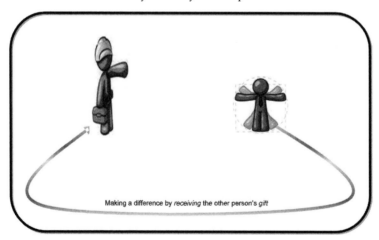

Making a difference by *receiving* the other person's *gift*

Figure 7.2 Receiving

It is fascinating to realise that what you like to give others based on your mission is usually what you would like to receive from others. How you manage others as an authentic leader is really how you want to be managed yourself. Compare your mission with the way you are being managed. Is it the same? Is it different? It is a good opportunity to discuss your mission with your manager or supervisor and tell her what leadership style you would like her to adopt. Regardless, it is interesting to ask your leader what her mission is. How would she like to see you improve yourself? And what would you think of, for example, asking your clients what their mission is? Sharing your mission with others creates a stronger bond. This is why we ask everyone to prepare and share their mission in teams.

When your gift is not received

It's annoying, it can hurt, but it's a part of life. You give something with the best intentions, but your gift is not wanted. Because your creation will not come to anything in the other person, you won't receive confirmation that you made a difference. You don't receive anything. The aim of authentic giving is not to receive something. If that is your goal, your behaviour is ego-driven. Giving is unconditional. You have thought about your mission, about the steps that have to be taken, your responsibilities. You therefore accept the resulting consequences (for better or for worse). If things are not received, there are only four questions you can ask authentically:

1. *Should I complain about it?* In the long-term this is not always the most tactful behaviour, but it sometimes feels good to get things off your chest.

2. *Should I act?* If you're going to deal with it, ask yourself how you can convey your mission to others in the future. Every gift not received will teach you how to do things differently. An important characteristic of authentic leaders is that they are immediately able to turn disappointment into an opportunity. Giving according to your mission does not stop because of an obstacle along the way.

3. *Should I lower my expectations?* If you accept it, this could mean you might revise your mission, or don't mind that some people don't embrace your mission.

4. *Should I leave?* If you are considering walking away, ask yourself if your mission will be better accomplished in another environment. It will be a wise decision if you realise your environment has no need for your mission, is continually obstructive, rejects your gifts or, for example, your company is pursuing a completely different mission. You're not walking away; you're simply choosing a new environment.

Receiving without self-sacrifice

Many people believe that you shouldn't derive any pleasure from the things you create. That it wouldn't be authentic if no self-sacrifice was involved. This view is understandable. After all, you do it for others, not for yourself. If you are concerned about your own happiness that would qualify as ego behaviour, wouldn't it? However, there is a big difference between wanting to position yourself and wanting personal happiness. I hope that everyone is, wants to be, or will be happy, and will get a lot of pleasure from this. Ego behaviour is just a way to feel good – or less bad – by positioning yourself. If you feel happy through your own actions, this doesn't explicitly mean that you are displaying ego behaviour, since this would mean you have to serve your environment at the expense of lifelong unhappiness and suffering. On the contrary, you can get an enormous amount of pleasure from the beautiful things you create authentically in the world around you. This will increase your motivation to create even more things. That is what you were put on earth for. I would really like to turn the proposition on its head. You are usually not authentic if a creation you want to bring to fruition doesn't make you feel good. The Nice One and the Adviser are good examples. The Nice One is trying to elevate others to a higher level but is not certain if the others like him. In itself, elevating others to a higher level doesn't give him an immediate sense of fulfilment. And the Adviser is not certain if the person he is giving advice to really needs him.

What *is* authentic is to consciously choose to make a sacrifice in order to create something you consider to be even more important than maintaining your own position. The sacrifice is therefore a consequence of a mission. For example, when a parent is prepared to lay down her life for her child the mission towards the child is more important than her own life. The parent will then have 'chosen' the consequences. An example in the world of business is stepping down for a younger manager who needs to develop further; or turning down your bonus to set an example for your staff when spending cuts are really necessary. You choose to make a sacrifice because, in doing so, something greater will be created. In short, (self-) sacrifice is not a condition for authentic behaviour, but could be a result.

Giving and receiving the best of yourself

Behaviour that stems from your mission doesn't only mean elevating others to a higher level. Authenticity includes giving yourself the best (see Figure 7.3). In fact, this is a requirement. If you're not able to invest in yourself and help yourself to develop further, it is terribly difficult to help others develop further from your authenticity, since you need to have something to give away if you want to give someone something. It is precisely when you have (a sense of your own) value that you can add value. Therefore, make sure you receive value. People who don't invest in themselves but nevertheless give a lot to others often do so from ego motives. They give in order to demand recognition. Therefore, make sure you continue to work on your personal growth and happiness in a structured manner. It also holds true here that the mission you direct towards others is also directed at yourself. The things you want to give others are the things you want to receive from others. In other words, a near-perfect closed loop is formed from your Authentic Leadership: you would like to give yourself and receive from yourself the things you want to give others and receive from others so that you can grow in the areas you want others to grow.

What is fantastic about authentic giving is that you don't lose what you give. When you impart knowledge to someone, you don't lose that knowledge. When you give someone love, you don't lose that love. The interesting thing is that your own value actually increases when another person receives your value, especially when this person reciprocates with their value. This applies to any environment you invest in. You will only become more self-confident when you see that you have a lot to give. Receiving is a basis for being able to give more. Give yourself the credit that you are due. It is terrible to think that you don't make a difference, that you are not recognised. That would be a pity for yourself and for others. Moreover, it simply isn't true. Your deepest self hides a wonderful and beautiful person who has much to give and can receive anything, from yourself and others. You may have lost this feeling temporarily. However, this doesn't mean that it's not there. You make a difference. Rediscover why!

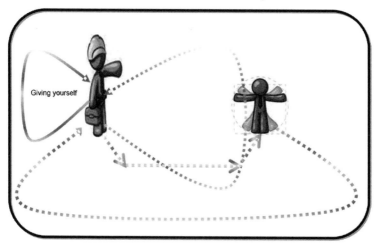

Figure 7.3 Giving yourself

People are sometimes afraid to be thought of as arrogant. They are actually afraid to be thrown out of the group (i.e. an ego issue). However, there is a big difference between being 'self-assured' and 'arrogant'. 'Self-assurance' concerns yourself, your self-awareness, your belief in your ability to deal with things and the value you assign to yourself. 'Arrogance' concerns how you position yourself in relation to others. If you are arrogant, you position yourself above others or pull others down. Someone who is very confident in himself is not bothered about positioning himself. He is simply convinced that he's capable of many things. And that's fine, since false modesty is not a virtue. Don't be afraid to invest in yourself, since this will benefit you and your environment.

In his inaugural address as president of South Africa, Nelson Mandela recited a poem by Marianne Williamson. They are fine words that give pause for thought:

Our deepest fear is not that we are inadequate

Our deepest fear is that we are powerful beyond measure

It is our LIGHT, not our darkness that most frightens us

We ask ourselves 'Who am I to be brilliant, gorgeous, talented, fabulous?'

Actually, who are you not to be?

Your playing small does not serve the world

There's nothing enlightened about shrinking

So that other people won't feel insecure around you

We are all meant to shine as children do

And as we let our own light shine

We unconsciously give other people permission to do the same

As we're liberated from our own fear,

Our presence automatically liberates others.

AUTHENTIC BEHAVIOUR – AN IN-DEPTH PERSPECTIVE

When do we display authentic behaviour?

We display authentic behaviour when we feel secure in a group. Because we're not concerned about our position, we can give ourselves completely to our mission. There is no need to call egos into play here. Incidentally, you should realise that you often behave authentically without being aware of it. You can see this in people who have a lot of experience in a certain area. The environment they operate in doesn't pose many threats and is therefore safe. They know exactly what to do. You feel safe when you feel completely accepted and are prepared to show your vulnerable side, your true self. This could be with good friends, or in a workshop where you are expected to be open, but also in a train compartment where you have a deep conversation with a fellow passenger, or the couple you met on holiday and got on so well with. What is interesting is that the safety in the latter two examples is not based on complete acceptance, since you don't know each other well, but on the fact that you will probably never see these people again. Your show of vulnerability has no further consequences, so the situation is safe. You should realise that your *selective perception* qualifies something as unsafe;

safety is not a precondition for authenticity. Later in this chapter I discuss how you can make an unsafe environment safe, so that you can behave authentically more often.

We show our authentic behaviour when a certain vision, mission or value drives our behaviour. Because you pursue a higher goal, your own position becomes less important. The safety you require becomes less of an issue. You recognise this safety in organisations where the vision, mission and values are crystal clear. Staff members therefore behave more authentically (without being aware of it). They have, as it were, committed themselves to this environment. If every staff member pursues the same goal, it is easier to confront each other. This results in an authentic and creative environment.

Does 'authentic' mean spontaneous, kind and nice?

'Authentic' is often used interchangeably with 'spontaneous'. However, as I interpret them, these are different concepts. Authentic behaviour does not have to be spontaneous. In fact, you can demonstrate rehearsed authentic behaviour. If you pursue a vision, you can consciously ask yourself what behaviour brings the best creation to fruition. You can also display extremely calculating behaviour during negotiations in order to try to make the best win–win deal. With authentic behaviour your creative motive takes over. You already saw in Chapter 5 that egos can be called into play spontaneously and subconsciously. We can therefore relegate statements such as 'Under pressure, you get to know someone's true nature' to the realm of fiction. The reality is that under pressure you get to know someone's successful egos. A display of authentic or ego behaviour could have been a very conscious choice. When you start to feel better and achieve better results from your mission, you will see that the authentic behaviour you display will be increasingly spontaneous and subconscious.

So, is authentic behaviour always kind and nice? Absolutely not! However, your positive intention always leads the way. Even when you want to put someone in her place because you think her behaviour is unacceptable, you can do this with a positive intention. Do you want to punish someone because she is guilty? Or do you want to draw someone's attention to the negative consequences of her behaviour and help her to better carry future responsibility by giving advice? You could call the latter 'authentic'. You are trying to elevate the person to a higher level. This doesn't mean that you have to deal with this person with kid-gloves. You can be very direct and harsh with someone as long as you and the other person are clear about your intention. So, don't think that authentic behaviour is just soppy and soft. On the contrary, living according to your mission means that you stray less from the path you want to follow. However, you may be more likely to part ways with employees who consistently obstruct your mission. And you lay off staff authentically, with a positive intention in mind. With regard to dismissal, there are a few good practical examples where employers and employees parted ways amicably because their visions or missions differed. Telling your board that you think your relationship leaves something to be desired, that you see concrete opportunities to improve it, is of course exciting and quite authentic. The trick is to keep communicating your positive intention to the group you are having problems with.

Behaving authentically towards another person could mean that you are demoting that person to a lower level. For example, if someone wants to hurt your child, and can only be stopped by using violence, you will do so. Is that authentic? After all, you are not automatically elevating this person to a higher level (whereas you are elevating your child). A complicated problem arises here: if someone stands in the way of your mission or vision, or if someone is a hindrance, you sometimes choose to demote the person concerned to a lower level since this is justified by a higher goal. In other words, you behave authentically towards the environment you want to elevate to a higher level (this could be any environment) until a crucial conflict arises between your visions and missions. Incidentally, this means that you can still deal with 'the victim' with a positive intention (in the example of dismissal, a positive intention is to ensure that the parties part ways 'amicably'). However, you haven't always got the time to come up with a good alternative, such as when your child is under threat.

Abundance or scarcity

An important reason to call an ego into play is the perception of scarcity, the notion that there is a shortage of something. This could be money, raw materials, career opportunities, time, love, etc. Because of scarcity, people feel justified in looking out for number one at the expense of others.

Egos often think in terms of scarcity. Scarcity as a norm often leads to selfish behaviour: you immediately take something before someone else takes everything. Of course, others will operate within the same framework and the negative self-fulfilling prophecy will be fulfilled. An interesting point is that we are even prone to turning a non-scarce item into a scarce one because of an inability to share. Authentic Leadership does not take scarcity as a starting-point, but rather the realisation that there is enough to go around: abundance. When you enter into negotiations authentically, with a positive intention in mind, this means that you are capable of sharing. You are prepared to receive and you are prepared to give. An outcome that maximises the benefits for both parties is to be preferred to an outcome that only benefits you. This is often referred to in literature as a 'win–win deal'. A win–win deal makes it possible to elevate both parties to a higher level. Those who can't share can't multiply. This also applies to negotiations. It appears that opposing views often hide a shared interest – an interest which offers much wider scope for healthy negotiations.

GIVING AND FORGIVING

Authentic behaviour concerns giving. You give something to a person and they are elevated to a higher level. Forgiving is one of the most important forms of authentic giving. It is good to think about this since hate and hard feelings are real energy killers.

A relationship can come under enormous pressure when you think that another person is 'guilty' of certain bad behaviour. For example, someone may have shamelessly insulted you at work. In the private sphere this could mean, for example, that your partner has been unfaithful. In other words, a disaster. All kinds of things take place in your inner world. You no longer trust the story in your head about this person because you feel that your old image is no longer correct. 'He is not the kind of person who would do such a thing' is replaced by 'He is the kind of person who would do such a thing.'

You may be familiar with the expression 'to forgive and forget', but it is nonsense to think that you can only forgive someone if you can forget the incident. Precisely because you can be really upset by a nasty incident that you can't forget, it is all the more important that you forgive. And when we say 'forgive', we don't mean 'Come on, it doesn't matter. I didn't mind.' No, when you forgive, you give something. But what?

The answer is to *once more put your trust* in the other person. You tell him implicitly that you trust he will stop this nasty behaviour. You tell him that you trust he will turn his feelings of guilt into responsibility to stop what he was doing. Forgiving someone is often the most impressive thing you can give another person.

To really put your complete trust in someone again is too much to ask of some people. Trust is often – especially in business contexts – regarded as something binary, as something that is either there or not. Fortunately, the idea of trust being binary is wrong. Giving trust is like a volume control; you can turn it up or down. You can trust someone to a greater or lesser extent. If someone has done something to you, your trust may slowly have to be restored. In that case, you can say that you are *trying* to forgive someone. In doing so, you express your intention to allow the (relationship of) trust to grow. You won't be able to completely forgive another person until trust has been fully restored. When you are ready, make this known. It will benefit the other person and it will benefit you.

Although forgiving is nice for the other person, it is sometimes even much more important for yourself. This really comes into play if some-one has done something that still really affects you. For example, a sup-plier may have cheated you. You will therefore never trust suppliers again, and it will be very difficult to make win–win deals. However, there are also very serious examples, such as rape, when someone has given up hope of ever having a healthy relationship again. You may feel that you can't develop further because of a particular incident and hold the other person responsible for the slow-down in your development. This is called complaining. If you continue to complain, you will make the other person responsible for your happiness. Incidentally, it is sometimes good to complain, since it may (still, for the time being) be too much of a burden to assume responsibility for your future. Moreover, it can feel better to project negative feelings and fears onto a guilty party. However, be aware of the consequences and accept them. If you are eventually able to forgive a person, this means that you will no longer hold the incident or the person responsible for your further development. In this case, forgiving means that you trust yourself to be responsible for your future. This doesn't mean of course that you have to approve of what someone did to you; that is not necessary to be able to forgive.

With forgiveness, it helps to think what the other person's *intention* was when she hurt you. Did someone hurt you intentionally, or was it an unfortunate combination of events? Can you blame someone or hold someone responsible for something that happened to you which she could not have foreseen? I don't think so. For example, you are accidentally hit by a bus after your boss sent you home early because you were tired. Quite awful for you, but it didn't enter into your boss's head that this might happen. When you realise this, it will be easier to forgive.

Things become more difficult when someone didn't intend to hurt you, but knew they were taking a certain risk. In the example of the child who, after a lot of practice, crosses a busy road for the first time and is hit by a car, it is my personal opinion that the parents have responsibility. Whether you (as the child) will be able to forgive them for this will depend on how carefully the risk assessment was made.

It is even more difficult when someone acted towards you with bad intentions, and actually intended to demote you to a lower level. It will then be very difficult to forgive this person. It is important in this case to make sure this person no longer has any control over your future. As long as you make the other person responsible for your future, you will remain dependent on him. Don't give him the satisfaction. You can, without forgiving, decide to be responsible for yourself and your future from now on.

If someone didn't intend to hurt you, it will be easier to forgive. It helps enormously if the guilty party apologises or asks for forgiveness. This indicates that the other person regrets her actions and realises that she was in the wrong. This could mean that the other person really takes responsibility to stop doing what she was doing. Someone might not be aware of the impact of their actions. In that case, you can still forgive.

If the other person shows no remorse whatsoever, it will be extremely difficult to forgive. However, you can decide that he is no longer responsible for your further development.

In practice

I meet many people in practice who come to realise that they hold a grudge against certain persons (e.g. their parents). They might think their parents are responsible for their lack of self-confidence, which meant they couldn't develop that quickly. It could be that the parents didn't stimulate the child enough, were too strict, never expressed their appreciation, were absent too often, etc. This image from the past is deeply imprinted in their inner world and has assumed a meaning of its own, in the form of 'My parents didn't think I was important enough, so I'm probably not that important'. It will come as a shock if you come to this realisation as an adult ('How could my parents have done this to me?', 'Aha, my parents are the reason I'm afraid to take risks!'). If you recognise this in yourself, you need to watch out. You are complaining that your environment is responsible. You should ask yourself what your parents' intention was. Did they hurt you intentionally? Did they know what they were doing to you? There was usually a positive intention behind their behaviour ('A strict upbringing makes for strong adults', 'Not too many compliments or they'll get big-headed'). Some parents believe these norms prepare a child for a bright future. Parents are often totally unaware that they sometimes have a negative effect on their children. This could be because they are led by their positive intentions, or because they can't see the consequences of their behaviour. This can in turn result from the way they were raised themselves, something they (subconsciously) project onto their own children, or because they really haven't the slightest idea that their behaviour could be harmful (i.e.

unconsciously incompetent). And then, sadly, there are parents who project their own frustrations onto their children. They are too preoccupied with themselves and don't care enough about their children's well-being. You should therefore think about your parents' intentions before you start to hold a grudge against them.

If you see that your parents had the right intentions, you will find it easier to forgive them. In fact, you might realise that you actually had no reason for holding something against them all this time. It could have been a story which you exaggerated and used subconsciously as an excuse not to take certain risks. If you realise this, it is more appropriate to apologise than to forgive.

If your parents or other significant adults had the wrong intentions, you may find it more difficult to forgive them. Try to understand them anyway. It might help you to put yourself in their position. You might be able to forgive them because you will become responsible for your future again, rather than blaming your upbringing. You're back in the driver's seat.

Be careful when you forgive others, especially parents. It is no small matter if, for example, your child appears on your doorstep after forty years to forgive you for your parenting. If, as the parent, you're not aware of any harm done, you will be completely shocked: 'Have you been living with this all these years? And I was the cause of the problem? That's awful!'

You should realise that you can also quietly forgive someone, without expressing it. What's most important about forgiving is that you take the driver's seat again, and don't let others have the responsibility for your further development. If you do want to talk about it, put the emphasis on what you would like to achieve in the future, instead of what went wrong in the past.

Asking for forgiveness, offering apologies

Now that we have discussed forgiveness, it also makes sense to see what you can do if you did something to another person. Rather than forgiving, this concerns asking for forgiveness. You authentically offer your apologies. This is what you give another person. Authentic giving is *unconditional*; you can't force someone to forgive you. You sometimes hear someone admitting to a mistake by saying 'You're right, I shouldn't have done that.' This isn't enough. Admitting a mistake is not the same as offering your apologies; you are not giving the other person anything since you are not offering anything. All the other person hears is your assessment, nothing more. She will therefore (subconsciously) be left feeling dissatisfied. Offering your apologies means telling someone that you are sorry about what you did. You might not have intended to hurt someone but you accept responsibility for doing so and assure them that you won't do it again. And you explain that you hope trust can be restored in the future. If you are forgiven then 'receive' this with thanks.

TRY THIS...

Is there somebody you haven't forgiven? Is this affecting you or holding back your development? If this is the case, ask yourself if it isn't time to forgive them. You can do this by talking to them or, alternatively, do it silently.

This sometimes concerns a deceased person. In such a case maybe you could write a letter. You could read it out loud to yourself or to a relative of the deceased person. Remember that you forgive with your head and your heart. The person you are forgiving doesn't have to be present.

Is there someone you would like to apologise to? If so, don't you think it's time to do so?

PROJECTING PROBLEMS ONTO THE AUTHENTICITY LAYER

If you can't solve a problem on the values layer because the answers you have found are still not at the correct level, the problem should be redefined again. So far the problems have been defined as:

- My environment is the problem (environmental layer).

- What should I do to solve my problem with my environment? What should I do to feel happy again? (behavioural layer).

- How should I influence my environment (to feel happy again)? (skills layer).

- Which stimulating or restrictive norm should take precedence in order for me to solve my problem with my environment? (norms layer).

- Which egos should I let go of or use to be able to properly solve my problem with my environment (so that I can feel happy again)? (ego layer).

- How should I behave towards my environment if I let myself be guided by my values (so that I can feel happy again)? (values layer).

The problem on the authenticity layer is redefined as:

What do I want to contribute to my environment if I let myself be guided by my mission? How can I elevate my environment to a higher level if I bring out the best in myself?

In your mission statement you described what it is you will contribute to this world, what value you wish to add to your environment. You know what it is you want to create in your environment. You have already determined that this is your sense of purpose, that this has a major influence on your sense of fulfilment. By thinking about how you would behave if you let yourself be guided by your mission, you will see that you make a different mental association. You will start to use a completely different part of your inner world. You will direct the association to the part where some visions and missions have been firmly established, and not so much to the parts where your egos are stored. I have already pointed out that authentic behaviour does not have to be spontaneous. When you are stuck in one of your egos, it will help to consciously switch from claiming (a position) to giving (see also Chapter 8).

If you can't immediately establish a link to your mission, ask yourself the following simple question: How can I elevate my environment to a higher level if I bring out the best in myself? This will enable you to make authentic mental associations, just as it does when you use your mission.

Therefore, in the example of the controlling boss, ask yourself the following two questions: What do I want to give my boss if I let myself be guided by my mission? How can I elevate my boss to a higher level? Imagine if the following were your mission: To let myself and my environment feel more fulfilled and be more successful. In that case, you will have a talk with your boss to find out what drives her, and then jointly examine how you can realise a form of collaboration that is agreeable to you both. It is good to be very open about your own mission here (by pointing out that you really want her to be successful and to feel good as well).

TIPS FOR RECOGNISING AUTHENTIC BEHAVIOUR

Apart from using your mission, there are other ways to quickly determine what your authentic behaviour would look like in a particular situation. These are useful tips, since they can easily be applied in consultations or negotiations. Some of these tips will crop up again in Chapter 8. However, you should realise that these tips are most effective if you have first thought about your mission.

1. Role model

   Think carefully about someone you regard as very strong and authentic. If you want to know what your authentic behaviour looks like in a particular situation, ask yourself 'What would my role model do?' A quick association and evaluation process will then take place in your inner world, producing, in general, very clear results.

   You can use a version of this role model for hierarchical problems. For example, if you have a conflict with your manager, it may not be safe to interact with her because of her position of power over you. The trick is to picture how you would act if the environment were safe. For example, ask yourself how you would react if you were your boss's boss. With a hierarchical problem, you can also try to imagine how your manager's best friend would react. Finally, it is nice to see yourself as a role model. With hierarchical problems, we sometimes ask leaders how they would behave if the problem was one of their staff members, rather than their manager. They usually give a very authentic example. We often see leaders behave more authentically towards their staff than towards their own managers. Incidentally, this can be explained by the fact that you know – consciously or subconsciously – that, as well as authentic authority, you also have power. Because you know this, I hope you will rarely have to wield your power. This works the other way round with your own manager. You know that your manager can ultimately use her power. This could (sub)consciously trigger a fear motive.

2. Financial independence

It appears that many people are not authentic because the possibility of being fired is always at the back of their minds. They therefore feel that they have to take everything that's dished out to them. In fact, they don't ask themselves what they really want. One way to remove this obstacle is to ask yourself what you would do if you had decided to keep your job *and* if you were financially independent.

3. Making an environment safe

You may feel that the person (or persons) you are speaking to are unsafe for you because you're not certain what attitude he has (or they have) towards you. This uncertainty may prompt you to call your egos into play. If you would nevertheless like to see what your authentic behaviour would look like, ask yourself the following question: What would you do if you were certain that the other person had your best interests at heart? You should realise that your perception of the environment as 'unsafe' is just a perception. You are in fact influencing your selective perception. Because you make the environment safe in your inner world, you have less need to call an ego into play.

4. The mirror

Stand in front of your mirror, quietly look at yourself for five seconds, then say your name and ask yourself 'What do I really want?' Look at yourself for a bit longer, listening carefully to the self-talk that comes into your head.

5. The best

   A very simple method for recognising your most authentic behaviour, one which goes to the heart of the matter, is to ask yourself 'What will I be able to contribute to my environment if I show the best and most admirable side of myself?'

6. Your values

   You saw in Chapter 6 that when you act according to your values, you usually behave authentically. Therefore, the problem on the values layer helps you to recognise your authentic behaviour: How should I behave towards my environment if I am led by my values (so that I can feel happy again)?

These are a few tips you can use to quickly recognise what your authentic behaviour would look like. If you eventually choose not to behave authentically, fine. You can choose from one of the following courses of action again: complain, act, lower your expectations or leave. You also have at least eight egos that might take over from your authentic self. Be aware of your options, make a conscious choice and accept the consequences.

Rule of thumb

To conclude this chapter, here is a rule of thumb for recognising the use of authenticity. Ask yourself what the underlying intention of your behaviour towards others is:

- If you intend to contribute something to your environment using your mission as the determining factor, your authenticity is the determining factor.

- If you intend to elevate your environment and yourself to a higher level, your authenticity is the determining factor.

SUMMARY

The authenticity layer is the deepest layer of your existence, the source from which everything emanates. Authenticity means genuineness and, therefore, reliability. Authentic behaviour is genuine since it arises from your true self rather than from your ego. You don't have to be labelled in any way since you already know who you are, what you stand for, and for what purpose you were put on this earth. Your deepest motive lies hidden within your authenticity: your mission, what you are going to contribute. Your authentic self's mission is to give the best of yourself to your environment. Giving is an essential concept here. Giving is unconditional. The reward of authentic behaviour is to make a difference. You achieve this by seeing the creation that stems from your mission. The reward is a very good feeling. When you defined your mission in this chapter, you established exactly what you want to create, or what you can give to your environment. You can have several missions, although they often come together in one comprehensive mission.

You can sum up Authentic Leadership as 'exerting influence with your mission in mind, in a genuine and reliable way', where your authentic behaviour gives you the best chance to achieve happiness and results. Someone who helps both herself and others to develop will find more happiness and greater results along her path than someone who only helps herself to develop. There is a kind of pattern: the more you experience the added value of your mission, the greater your sense of fulfilment.

A vision can be defined from a mission. You define a vision by asking yourself what the environment will look like after a few years if your mission was always the determining factor. The good thing about a vision is that it is easy to convey to others. Once you have defined a vision, you can make a step-by-step plan for how you can realise it. You have a mission, you create a vision. Then you focus on the here and now throughout the step-by-step plan. It is important here not to be afraid to receive gifts from others. By being able to receive, you make it possible for the other person's creations to be accepted, thereby sharing the good feeling.

Any insights into your personal mission can also be applied to your team's or organisation's mission.

Sacrifice is not a condition for authentic behaviour, but could be a result. Precisely because you think you are valuable, you can pass on much value to others. Therefore, make sure you also continue to invest in yourself.

You behave authentically when you feel secure in a group. Egos are not needed then. You recognise safety in organisations where the vision, mission and values are crystal clear. You may behave authentically towards a person while demoting him to a lower level. You will behave authentically towards the environment you want to elevate to a higher level.

Forgiving is a form of authentic giving. When you forgive, you give back your trust. If you can forgive someone, this means that you no longer hold the incident or the person responsible for your further development. You can also ask for forgiveness, or offer your apologies. Authentic leaders can admit their mistakes and offer their apologies. Their positive intention to do things better in the future strengthens them here.

The problem on the authenticity layer is defined as: What do I want to contribute to my environment if I let myself be guided by my mission? How can I elevate my environment to a higher level if I bring out the best in myself?

Tips for recognising your authentic behaviour:

- Role model: What would my role model do in a particular situation?

- Financial independence: What would I do if I had decided to keep my job or if I were financially independent?

- Making an environment safe: How would I behave if I was certain that the other person had my best interests at heart?

- The mirror: What do I really want?

- The best: What will I be able to contribute to my environment if I show the best and most admirable side of myself?

- Your values: How should I behave towards my environment if I am led by my values in my behaviour (so that I will feel happy again)?

8
From ego to authenticity

In this chapter I will first establish the main differences between ego and authenticity before further elaborating the information from Chapters 5 and 7 to be able to move from ego to authenticity.

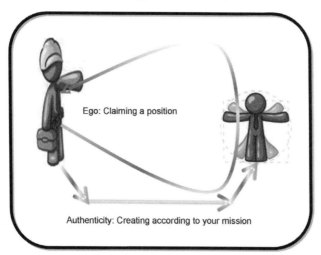

Figure 8.1 Ego and authenticity

DIFFERENCES BETWEEN EGO AND AUTHENTICITY

Examples where ego and authenticity look very similar

Behaviour can look the same, whether it has arisen from the ego or the authenticity layer. Characteristic examples of normal and ego behaviour are given for each ego below.

Ego 1: Sally the Show-off tells of a positive experience in order to receive praise.
Authentic Anthony tells of a positive experience so that others can learn from it.

Ego 2: Simon the Soloist turns down offers of assistance because he's afraid of falling off his pedestal.
Authentic Alice turns down offers of assistance because she likes to do the job herself.

Ego 3: Violet the Victim says she's not to blame in order to get herself off the hook.
Authentic Andrew places responsibility where it belongs.

Ego 4: Dennis the Dodger keeps his mouth shut in the group because he's afraid of making a mistake.
Authentic Alberta keeps her mouth shut in the group so that someone else can have a say.

Ego 5: Susan the Sweet Talker pays a compliment in order to receive recognition in return.
Authentic Adam pays a compliment in order to help someone develop.

Ego 6: Elroy the Envious puts someone else's success into perspective in order to receive more attention himself.
Authentic Anna puts someone else's success into perspective in order to convince people that they can also achieve that success.

Ego 7: Patricia the Paternalist gives advice in order to make people dependent on her.
Authentic Arthur gives advice in order to make others independent.

Ego 8: David the Demolisher imposes a resolution because his leadership could be called into question if there were a discussion.
Authentic Alex imposes a resolution because customers wouldn't receive prompt service if a discussion were held.

When you examine these examples, you see that the behaviour that arises from your ego can closely resemble the behaviour that comes from your authenticity. An important similarity is that both behaviours have the same reward: making a difference. The desired result of both behaviours is proof that you have a right to be here, that you have a right to exist. The main distinction is that, with ego behaviour, you make a difference in claiming a position from another person, while, with authentic behaviour, you make a difference by creating something based on your mission.

It is Sally the Show-off's intention to be labelled in a certain way, to position herself, while authentic Anthony wants to elevate the other person to a higher level. The difference lies in the intention behind the behaviour. When egos are let down, they find this very annoying. Their position will immediately be the subject of discussion, or so they think. However, authentic people will immediately look for a solution. They are continually trying to give the best they've got so even if they don't achieve their (intended) results, they will look for new ways to try again – without blaming themselves. After all, what should they blame themselves for? You can't do any more than give your best with a positive intention.

Conclusion: the main difference between authentic behaviour and ego behaviour is *the intention behind the behaviour* (see Table 8.1). Are you led by your mission or by your position?

Table 8.1 *Differences between authenticity and ego*

Authenticity	Ego
You are led by your mission	You are led by your position
You are somebody	You want to be labelled in a certain way
It's genuine	It's a trick
Position is unimportant	Position is important
Action is the determining factor	Reaction is the determining factor

Authenticity	Ego
You are responsible for the success, you lead the way and are thus not dependent on others	Success can be attributed to the other person's reaction, the other person leads the way, so that you become dependent on others
The creation motive leads the way	The fear motive (usually) leads the way
Realise a positive consequence	Often avoid a negative consequence
Intention: you and the environment grow	Intention: personal growth
You create a positive drive in others	You create potential fears in others
Inspires others to also display authentic behaviour	Inspires others to also display ego behaviour
Results in greater commitment from others	Results in less commitment from others
You give unconditionally	You give conditionally
You receive a lot	You claim a lot
The other person gives you something in return	You claim something from another person
Strengthens relationships	Keeps relationships superficial
You feel fulfilled while carrying out an activity	You feel fulfilled when you acquire a position
Generates energy	Costs energy
Leads to optimal happiness and optimal results	May lead to good results and happiness
Is used in safe environments (I can be myself)	Is used in unsafe environments (I can't be myself since something unpleasant could happen)

Authenticity	Ego
Is a matter of 'wanting to'	Is a matter of 'having to'
Driven by internal norms and values	Driven by external norms
Is not done against your will	Is done against your will
There is a long-term motive (mission) and vision	There is a short-term motive (position)
Works in the long-term	Only works in the short-term
Does not work immediately	Works immediately
Is lasting	Has immediate effect, but must be continually reaffirmed and is therefore not lasting
Happiness and attention lie in the present	Happiness and attention lie in the future
Positive self-fulfilling prophecy: creation is fulfilled	Potential negative self-fulfilling prophecy: fears come true
Reasoning from abundance	Reasoning from scarcity
The main reason you're here	A good way to make sure that you can stay here
Lets you live	Lets you survive
Focuses on effort (you will fail if you don't give the best you've got)	Focuses on results (you will fail if you don't achieve results)
Focuses on 'being'	Focuses on 'having'

Focus on effort or results

You have seen that your authenticity focuses on effort and your ego on results. However, as previously pointed out, the reality is slightly more complicated than this implies. 'Authentic' doesn't mean that results are unimportant. You and every staff member should be very clear about the objective (or vision). As an Authentic leader, you're not going to put up with staff members who repeatedly fail to achieve the intended results. The claim 'But I did my best' simply won't wash. The question is not whether someone did their best, but whether someone *really* brought out their very best, was fully committed, and did everything to the best of their ability.

Once the objective has become clear, the focus lies in the present. You continually bring out the best in yourself. It makes you feel good to lose yourself in the creation process. You enjoy every creation you bring about along the way. If the objective is not achieved, that's annoying, but not blameworthy. You can't give more than the best you've got. You have no alternative but to make a thorough assessment and learn from the experience so that you can do things differently in future or revise your objectives.

Your ego works differently. When you act according to your ego, you focus exclusively on your objective: 'If I don't achieve my objective, I have failed, and that's bad for my position.' This means you can't start enjoying yourself until you have achieved your objective. The effort is neither here nor there and it's the results that count. But this is just not very practical. The one can't do without the other, i.e. you can only influence how well you achieve your objective when you actually put the effort in. Some leaders try to achieve their objectives by putting as little effort in as possible. That is bad model behaviour. I recommend that such leaders are either promptly given training or replaced. At the very least, they should revise their objectives since, in the long-term, people don't like to achieve results without making any effort. They experience fewer happy moments. They don't feel challenged and are not growing. Because there's nothing to be proud of, they seek their happiness elsewhere. But make no mistake, a focus on effort does not mean that leaders have to do everything themselves.

People often feel they have failed if they haven't achieved a certain result. They blame themselves for all kinds of things. As a leader, it is worth considering casting the idea of failure in a different light. Failure may not be reflected in the end result, but in the effort. It is of course disappointing if you have failed to achieve a result, but the real question is whether you actually have given it your best shot. If that is the case, all you can do is learn how to do things better next time. Don't blame yourself too much. It could be that you're not the right person for the job. In that case, make sure that, with the right amount of effort, others will be able to achieve the results. Don't just assess the results, but also the quality of the effort. It's something you have direct control over.

Having and being

The question is whether you want to *be* somebody (authentic) or whether you want to *have* something so that you are labelled as somebody (ego) and can position yourself in a certain way. Things are fairly straightforward in the early stages of our development. Your environment uses external norms to tell you what is expected of you and what shape your future should take. You really don't have to think about this. In the West, this often means that you are thought to be somebody if you've got something or have achieved something. Over the years, you work towards getting a good education, a partner, children, a job, a home, a car, income and status. Your vision was clear but its realisation was a challenge. Apart from enjoying your creation, you (subconsciously) aspire to 'having' a lot, which makes you feel like you really are somebody. That's all very well, but the problem is that the joy of 'having' loses its charm after a while. The thrill wears off at an ever faster rate and feels less intense. I often come across this in practice. People who realise they've got everything their heart desires, but who feel ever unhappier. 'What else would I like to have?' They try to find the answer in the 'having', yet that no longer really helps. This often sets in as you reach middle age. Those who still then take the path of 'having' try to find the answer in a cool car, a motorbike or a new partner. Others realise that they are actually entering an interesting stage in their life: the 'being' stage. 'Who am I really?' That's a good question, at the right time. You have a rich past, have developed your personality and egos, have achieved your initial objectives, are able to cope with set-backs; you have a lot. You now enter a stage where you become aware of who you are and for what purpose you were put on this earth, that is, what your mission is. *Consciousness becomes being in a state of awareness.* You 'are' somebody now, so you don't need to 'have' so many things to prove it.

Authenticity and ego can alternate

You become aware that ego and authenticity can alternate quickly in a conversation and that an ego can also be used for strategic reasons to support a mission. In any case, it is important for you to make a clear distinction between authentic behaviour and ego behaviour. Below you will find four examples used in this book where authenticity and ego seem to alternate:

1. Behaving authentically towards another person could mean that you are demoting her to a lower level. The victim of your action is not very likely to recognise the authenticity of your behaviour.

2. When you move through the seven layers of authenticity to environment and behaviour, you automatically come across your ego layer. You actually use your ego all the time, even in accomplishing your mission. *When you do this consciously, you use* your ego authentically. You use, as it were, your ego's strength to achieve a higher goal. This is called '*strategic use of egos*'. For example, your mission within your working environment is to help your staff to develop. Imagine having someone on your staff who is being held back by all kinds of barriers which you think will automatically disappear if you give him a nudge in the right direction. In that case, it is authentic to use the Powerful One to push him through his barriers. The staff member's personal growth was the guiding force. You only used your ego as a means to an end. An example in the home situation is to use the Powerful One to impress on your child that she really needs to look carefully before crossing a busy street. Your mission towards your child is supported through your ego.

3. It sometimes seems as if you want to label yourself in a certain way, rather than wanting to be labelled in a certain way by another person. In that case, it does not appear to be an ego issue. However, when you look again, you realise that you are going back to a situation in the past when another person labelled you in a certain way.

4. You feel incredibly happy when your creation is well received. Things are more complicated when you create something authentically but your creation is not well received by the other person. Imagine hav-

ing brought out the best in yourself to advise another person, and this person reacts by saying 'That wasn't at all useful. Some help you are!' You could react authentically by telling the other person that this was the best you had to offer and that it is unfortunate that it wasn't useful. You could then look for other ways to support him or wish him success in finding a proper solution for his problem. You could also be very disappointed. It will then look as though you gave the advice to 'be indispensable', i.e. ego. This does not necessarily have to be the case. You may have sincerely intended to elevate the other person to a higher level when you gave that advice. The other person's reaction is a new development that has no bearing on your intention. The question now is how to deal with this new development: authentically (see above) or based on your ego: 'Then jolly well work it out yourself!' However, this does not detract from your original intention.

Rule of thumb

To determine whether behaviour is authentic, it is wise to look for your deepest motive. You can do this by simply asking yourself why you behave in a certain way. The rule of thumb for distinguishing ego behaviour from authentic behaviour is to ask yourself what your intention is: 'Do I want to help my environment to grow or do I want to position myself?'

If you intend to elevate your environment to a higher level or to contribute something so that your mission is the determining factor, your authenticity is the determining factor.

If you intend to position yourself in relation to another person or 'to be labelled in a certain way' by others, your ego is the determining factor.

TRY THIS...

Look at the decisions you made last week based on your ego and the decisions you made from your authenticity.

FROM EGO TO AUTHENTICITY

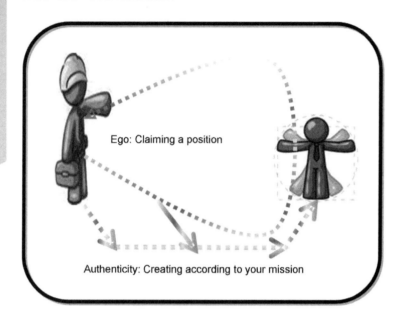

Figure 8.2 From ego to authenticity

You were put on this earth as an authentic being. You develop your egos so that you can hold your own in unsafe environments. Without being aware of it, you use your egos ever more because they bring you success. You have now reached the stage where you need to use your egos less so you can show more of your authentic self. This allows you to experience an even greater sense of fulfilment and to become more successful. Feeling the negative consequences of using your ego can also be a reason for moving from ego to authenticity.

A certain norm you follow in respect of an incident in your environment brings out an ego. This means that when you change the norm, you also change the way you use your ego. If you are in doubt as to what's best for you in a certain situation, ego or authenticity, you will do well to use the six-step analysis set out in the next section in order to *set norms for* and *compare* the various rewards, rather than the environment.

Analysis

Chapter 5 showed you how to carefully weigh up whether you should let your ego lead the way. You can do this by asking yourself what you stand to gain from using your ego:

- Reward: You realise … (e.g. position)

- You prevent … (e.g. loss of position)

- Costs: It will cost me … (e.g. the creation does not come to fruition)

- I risk … (e.g. a negative self-fulfilling prophecy)

If you decide to overrule your ego following this analysis, it is important to determine what the reward would be if you let your authenticity lead the way. To this end, first determine what your authentic behaviour looks like. You can do this by addressing the problem defined on the authenticity layer:

What do I want to contribute to my environment if I let myself be guided by my mission? How can I elevate my environment to a higher level if I bring out the best in myself?

- Role model: How would your role model, the boss's boss or your best friend deal with it?

- Financial independence: What would I do if I had decided to keep my job *and* if I were financially independent?

- Making an environment safe: What would you do if you were certain that the other person had your best interests at heart?

- The mirror: What do I really want?

- The best: What will I be able to contribute to my environment if I show the best and most admirable side of myself?

Now describe what you will stand to gain from this:

- Reward: You realise … (e.g. creation/mission)

- You prevent … (e.g. the creation from coming to fruition)

- Costs: It will cost me … (e.g. time and attention)

- I risk … (e.g. becoming too reckless)

Now compare these results with the results of Step 1 and decide whether you want your ego or mission to drive your behaviour.

When you behave authentically, explicitly tell the other person which positive intention lies behind your behaviour. By expressing your positive intention, you make the environment safer for yourself and for others, enabling them to show more of their authentic selves. If there is a risk that the environment is about to become unsafe again reiterate your positive intention. It also helps to simply say that you think it's exciting to identify the potential risks, yet you have still opted to let your positive intention take the lead. You are in fact identifying your fear and creation motives. This influences the other person's perception ('It's quite brave of her to go through with it despite her fears'). You can usually count on the other person's understanding and compassion.

Identifying your fears and your desired creation

The aim of this analysis is to be more in control of whether you want your ego or your authenticity to lead the way. If you decide on ego behaviour, then that's fine. You will have consciously weighed up the pros and cons and taken responsibility for certain behaviour, accepting its positive and negative consequences.

In general, you will see that authentic behaviour eventually produces the greatest rewards, especially if you have similarly had to weigh things up in the past and your subsequent experiences were positive. The positive self-fulfilling prophecy does the rest. Eventually you will notice that you behave authentically without extensively analysing it and being ever more unaware of it. At most, you will use the tips for recognising and giving concrete form to your authentic behaviour.

TRY THIS...

Analyse the eight ego examples given earlier in this chapter using the analysis framework above.

Take more risks

In short, you can move from ego to authenticity by following two steps in your mind:

1. How can I elevate my environment to a higher level if I bring out the best in myself?

2. Express this positive intention to the people around you and just do it!

Reflect on the last three words: just do it! You will sometimes have lingering doubts as to whether your environment is safe enough to be yourself. People often see the dangers before they see the opportunities for creation. It sometimes seems as if we have a tendency towards negativity. Try making the following remark to a few people: 'That's a nice shirt, but your shoes are a bit odd.' You will see that most people will focus on the comment about the shoes, the threat, but completely forget what you said about the shirt. It's not so strange that we have this tendency; fear exerts itself more directly than creation. People should be quickly made to feel secure otherwise they will not be able to bring about any creation. This is partly why you may decide to play it safe and call your ego into play. I encourage you to take more risks and show your authenticity. Things should be given a chance to succeed. Here's an interesting thought experiment that might help you in your deliberations:

- What do you feel is the probability of things going wrong? (I often hear 10%.)

- Aha ... so that means a 90% chance of success!

- What do you feel is the probability that you will be able to save your skin if things go wrong? (I often hear 90% here.)

AUTHENTIC LEADERSHIP

- Aha … so that means that, with a 10% chance of things going wrong, at the end of the day you will only suffer 10% damages!

- In other words, the probability that you will maintain your position is 99%!

This strange little exercise will lead you to take a more balanced view of the risks of authenticity. If you choose to behave authentically and others react negatively, you will have the opportunity to learn that you can cope with this. 'The fear of suffering is worse than the suffering itself'.

Your selective perception of an unsafe situation is often at odds with reality. You sometimes think people are taking too much notice of you but people are not always trying to label you. Try to get your self-talk under control (if necessary, use the examples of positive self-talk in Appendix 2 for this). This will help you to push your ego into the background and give your authenticity more room.

If you have the courage to behave authentically you may find that your authenticity has the impact needed at a particular point in time. Because this increases your self-confidence, you will be able to take greater risks in other situations. Don't forget that stepping out of your comfort zone always involves some stress. That's just the way things are. It is not called a comfort zone for nothing! However, if you succeed, your sense of fulfilment will be huge.

TRY THIS...

Look at how you worked out the last exercise and decide if you still dare to risk turning ego decisions into authentic decisions.

Review the decisions you have to make next week and analyse whether you can let your authenticity lead the way. Examine the results of your decisions the following week.

Dealing with other people's egos

Your authenticity is put nicely to the test when you are confronted with the exaggerated egos of other people. This is especially the case when they aim to lower your position. You may feel the urge to bring out your own exaggerated egos to prevent this happening, since one ego triggers another. The trick now is how to deal with this authentically. The interesting thing is that, once you have come to grips with the eight different egos, you will automatically feel how the other person is trying to *reposition* himself. He might pull you up in order to improve his own situation (the Sweet Talker!) or he might pull you down to assert his authority (the Demolisher!). It's the shoebox with the two balloons all over again: if one balloon is inflated, the other will immediately feel the pressure mount.

Realise that the other person has found it necessary to use his egos. This could be a subconscious mechanism. Alternatively, he could see you as an unsafe person. Therefore, first try to make the environment safe for him by continuing to behave authentically. Don't get involved in this *scramble for positions*, but cast aside your own exaggerated ego for the time being.

If the other person's ego keeps playing up, you could explicitly point out your positive intentions to the other person. This could mean, for example, that you highlight your common goal or interest, or explain your values or mission. If the person's ego continues to dominate the conversation, and you notice that this gets in your way or that of the goal, use the feedforward model to elevate the collaboration to a higher level. In any case, it is very important not to immediately get involved in this scramble for positions. If the other person sees that you really want to give the best you've got, his ego will, in general, recede into the background.

In short, it comes down to the following: imagine there is a problem and you are confronted with another person's exaggerated ego:

- Be aware that you are regarded as an unsafe person.

- You will (subconsciously) react from your own ego (one ego triggers another); that's fine, but do it consciously.

- Dispel fears by: (1) reacting from your values; (2) reacting from your mission (authenticity triggers authenticity).

You can also react very specifically to another person's exaggerated variant. You should first realise that another person's exaggerated ego wants to reposition itself. If the other person holds that position, there will not be as much need to call an ego into play.

- A Show-off wants an elevated position. Give him this position by expressing admiration and ask him to provide input.

- A Soloist wants to show that she can do it all on her own. Admire this and ask her for help so that you can solve the problem together.

- A Victim does not want to be blamed. Tell him you're aware that he already carries a lot of responsibility and that this isn't about who's to blame, but about a future-oriented solution for a problem. Ask for help.

- The Dodger doesn't want to attract any attention. Admire her modesty and ask her opinion about how you could solve the problem.

- The Sweet Talker wants to be recognised by you. Thank him for the nice compliments and see how you can solve the problem together.

- The Envious One does not want to give you any credit. Tell her you really need her help.

- The Paternalist wants to feel needed. Show your appreciation of his commitment and ask him to advise you on how you can further solve the problem by yourself.

- The Demolisher wants to be respected. Admire her strength and candour and ask her for advice.

The above examples show that you can ask for help. At times this means calling on another person's hidden mission. The danger of the above examples is that they can be very manipulative. This only works if your admiration and request for assistance are sincere. If you express admiration in order to manipulate the other person, he will sense this and resort to even more ego behaviour and rightly so, because you have become an unsafe person.

TRY THIS...

In the weeks ahead, try to help someone to move from ego to authenticity. Only do this when you know it will really benefit someone.

Egos form an integral part of you

When you have switched from ego to authenticity, you will become increasingly enthusiastic. You move on and focus on the many opportunities which you can still create in your life. However, after some time, you may suddenly find that your egos are playing up again. You then ask yourself if you've learned anything at all; some people try to get rid of their egos because they think that ego behaviour is an admission of weakness and that it suits them less and less. They have also experienced how strongly they have developed by being more authentic. There seems to be no place for egos any more. I don't think this is how it works. You're lucky this is not how it works! You had, and still have, an ego for a reason. It ensures that you survive in unsafe environments. This book may have opened your eyes to the fact that you may have called your exaggerated egos into play too often in the past, although there was really no need to. Because of the successes you achieved with your ego in the past, you may have thought this was your true self. You have passed that stage and you will remain past it. You have, as it were, put your authentic self back in the driver's seat and relegated your egos to the back seat. However, if you perceive your environment as unsafe, you will see your egos suddenly grab the wheel back from you. They will try to save you again. And you may thank your egos for this. The entire process is repeated in the new situation: you consciously start to recognise your ego, analyse what you stand to gain from this and then consciously determine what your authentic behaviour looks like in this new situation, analyse what you stand to gain from this and then finally make a decision. The rules for moving from ego to authenticity remain the same. You can compare this to a computer game. You learn the rules. Then, after some time, you jump from Level 1 to Level 2. Level 2 is more difficult, although the rules are the same. Your growth is reflected in your ability to play the game authentically with the same rules at an ever higher level. Your growth is not reflected in the fact that you have to get rid of your egos, but in the fact that you have less need of your egos in increasingly difficult or unsafe environments. You expand your comfort zone. However, your egos will briefly reappear at every new step. And that's fine.

TRY THIS...

Ask yourself what personal growth you have experienced. To answer this question, look at those situations where you would have used your egos in the past, but where you now behave authentically. Also make a note of the situations where you still call your ego into play. After some time, you will see that you now approach situations that used to trigger your egos ever more authentically. And that is something you can be proud of.

SUMMARY

In this final chapter you learned how to move from ego behaviour to authentic behaviour. Such a move is desirable because it will enable you to become more successful and fulfilled. The differences between ego and authenticity were therefore dealt with first. The main difference is the intention behind your behaviour. Is your mission the determining factor, or is your position the determining factor? If you intend to contribute something to your environment using your mission as the determining factor, your authenticity is the determining factor. If you intend to elevate your environment and yourself to a higher level, your authenticity is the determining factor. If you intend to position yourself in relation to another person or to be 'labelled' in a certain way by others, your ego is the determining factor. Both motives can serve you well, as long as you're aware of them. You should realise that ego behaviour and authentic behaviour can quickly alternate.

When you move through the seven layers from the centre outwards, you will automatically come across your ego layer. It is up to you to decide whether or not to use your ego to accomplish your mission. You can use your ego's strength to achieve a higher goal. This is 'calling your ego into play for strategic reasons'.

In short, you can follow two steps to move from ego to authenticity:

1. How can I elevate my environment to a higher level if I bring out the best in myself?

2. Express this positive intention to the people around you and just do it! Decide on this if your analysis shows that the benefits outweigh the costs.

Risk behaving authentically more often. You can't do any more than give the very best you've got. This is of course even more difficult when you're confronted with another person's irritating ego. However, it is worth realising that the decision to let your ego or your authenticity lead the way is ultimately yours, no one else's.

You can influence another person's egos by dispelling her fears through reacting from your own values or your own mission or by giving the other person recognition for the desired position and asking for help. Always do this for the right reasons otherwise it will have the opposite effect.

Your egos form an integral part of you. They automatically reappear when your environment becomes too unsafe. That's not a problem, egos benefit you, but you should not let them get the better of you. The rules for moving from ego to authenticity remain the same, no matter how unsafe the environment is. Your growth is reflected in the fact that you have less need of your egos in increasingly difficult or unsafe environments, and not in the fact that you need to get rid of your egos.

Conclusion

You have completed a long journey and have become acquainted with all seven layers of the model. I hope you never faltered and that you will never give up. There is much to do in this world. You have this magnificent authentic power to create beautiful things. It is waiting there to be released, over and over again. You have encountered several problems along the road as well as learning new ways to deal with them.

If we were in a café waiting for our drinks, we could strike up a conversation. You could tell me about the environments you spend time in, what you do for a living, what skills you need to do that job, when things are good, how other people might see you, what you stand for in life and what your contribution to this world will be. Well, that definitely makes it more than one drink's worth.

Exploring further on the website

In fact, after reading this book and working through the exercises, you can train yourself and others to deal with a variety of problems. You have learned on what layer particular problems belong and how you can solve those problems on that layer. You have also discovered that a problem on one layer may have originated from a deeper layer. It is now important that you start practising with all kinds of problems, so that you learn to handle the problems you come across.

On the website (www.authentiekleiderschap.nl/en) you will find examples of missions and a few articles that may inspire you. You can download files and listen to a synopsis of the book. I would really encourage you to visit the site. Also share your knowledge with others and with us (info@authentiekleiderschap.nl). We welcome the opportunity to learn from you. Or follow us on Twitter (@Authleadership or @basblekkingh, my personal account). You can also find us on Facebook under 'Authentic Leadership'. You will discover how rewarding it is to share your wisdom and to receive wisdom from others. In Appendix 6 I have included a drawing we use to explain our philosophy. It may help you when passing our ideas on to others.

Where does Authentic Leadership lead?

Imagine …

- If you lived according to the art of Authentic Leadership.

- That you are always able to give others the best you've got.

- That others receive this and become happier and more successful as a result.

- That you get a lot of pleasure from other people's development.

- That others also want to give you and others the best they've got.

- That you and others are capable of receiving this, which increases enjoyment and success.

- That others get a lot of pleasure from your development.

- That an increasing number of people will discover this and do this too.

This will surely result in a world where everyone is happy and successful.

A view of humanity and a view of life to which I will happily commit!

Have a good journey!

As you move closer towards Authentic Leadership, you will notice that you arouse people's interest because they see that you're becoming ever more successful and fulfilled. It's a nice idea to bring others (the people around you, or perhaps all the staff members of your company) along on your journey. You might even make this part of your mission. The trick is then to pass on the insights you have gained to others. You now have enough information to be able to provide guidance. Teach them the language of Authentic Leadership, discover each other's missions and three core values, have a laugh about one another's egos, share insight into restrictive and stimulating norms, pass on the key skills. You should realise here that true leaders don't create followers, but authentic leaders. Don't force others into thinking that authenticity is better for them. The most you can do is to encourage people to think about certain issues. If you push someone too much, you will become a norm-setter, and people will be quick to dismiss you as a Paternalist. The greatest reward would be for other people to be inspired by your model behaviour, or for the people around you to become more successful and fulfilled. There could also come a time when someone eventually sees the disadvantages of using an ego and becomes more receptive to self-reflection. You could play a role here. If a person doesn't feel any need whatsoever to dig deeper, the best you can do is pass on your insights to him or her so that they can support others.

In fact, Authentic Leadership has the same central message as most of the world's cultures: ensure your own happiness and, at the same time, make sure that you contribute to other people's happiness. Try to see other cultures and people in this light. And let's not try to impose rigorous, restrictive norms which detract from the essential beauty of cultures and people. People are closer to you than you might think. All individuals, teams and organisations have something beautiful: their authenticity. I would like to encourage you to create as many authentic leaders as possible. I leave it up to you how you should go about this, but I would be very interested to hear about your experiences. Share them with us, so that we may be empowered to gain new experiences, which we in turn will be able to share with you.

My dear Authentic colleague, I wish you happiness and success.

A fairy tale

Once upon a time, an elf was born. She grew up to be beautiful and radiated light. Most people got a warm, expansive feeling just from looking at her. However, some people were afraid of her. They felt that her light shone too brightly, as though with it she could see right through them. In order to dim her light they threw mud at her. This made the elf very sad. She hired eight guards to shield her from the mud. Outwardly, the guards looked very much alike, except that one was wearing a clown's nose, one was swinging a large club, one was carrying a shield and one had a megaphone through which he kept shouting at everyone to stop throwing mud. Each guard had a role to play. And the remarkable thing was that each was good at throwing the mud back. This cordon of guards was convenient for the elf. She was no longer being hit by lumps of mud. The guards shielded her from everything and her light could shine again.

But after a few years, she became lonely. She no longer saw the good people. It was only the guards who still had contact with people and it was their duty to keep them away from the elf. Her light only shone on the backs of the guards and didn't reach the people at all any more. She could no longer see the smiling faces of the happy ones or how the people who warmed themselves in her light were growing.

No, the guards weren't the answer. She wanted to re-establish contact with the people. So the elf went over to the guards and looked over their shoulders at the people standing there. Some people were eyeing the guards curiously while waiting for the elf to reappear, others had mud in their hands and were ready to throw it. She took a good look at the mud-slingers and suddenly saw something else. A light flickered and then vanished. Look! There it was again. The elf wanted to look into this but when she tried to walk past the guards they said 'Stop! Don't go outside, it's too dangerous. Have you forgotten about the mud? It will only make you sad.' Well, they had a point. So the elf turned back. But as she did so, she decided that she was tired of being lonely. She turned round and went over to the guards again. 'Say, guards, I'd really like to thank you. You've been looking after me so well for so many years. I have trusted you all this time and you have made me feel very secure. But now I'd like to get to know the outside world, because I saw a very beautiful light behind the mud-slingers. I'd like to see it up close.' 'It's just a ploy to draw you out. Don't let it fool you,' said one of the guards. The elf thought about this and then said 'I've got an idea. I'm much bigger now, so a lump of mud won't kill me. My light's strong enough. However, they could suddenly start to throw so much mud that I might need you again. What if you were to walk behind me, staying really close. You would then be able to come to my rescue if they start throwing too much mud.' The guards thought this was a good idea. And off they went, in single file, the elf in front, on the way to that beautiful light behind the mud-slingers.

Many people were happy to see the elf again. How her light had intensified! A few mud-slingers dropped their mud because they suddenly felt so much warmth that they were convinced there couldn't be any danger. Every now and then, though, somebody was still throwing mud. If somebody threw a small lump of mud, the elf just brushed it off and walked on regardless. And if large lumps of mud were thrown, a guard would quickly throw himself in front of her. And when the danger was over, he stepped back into line. After a while, she stood facing eight people with mud in their hands. They were guards too. She noticed that these guards looked a bit like hers. One of them wore a clown's nose, another one was carrying a club, another one … 'Stop, that's as far as you can go,' said the guards. 'You may not go any further, you're dangerous.' 'Who's there?' said a lovely voice behind the guards. The voice came from the same direction as the light the elf had seen. 'An odd-looking trouble-maker with a large number of guards,' answered a guard. 'Where's that beautiful warm light coming from?' said the voice, which sounded closer than before. 'It's a crazy elf,' answered the guard. 'An elf?' At that point, a beautiful elf appeared between two guards. The elves looked at each other. It seemed as if the light of one elf intensified the light of the other. They felt incredibly happy and immediately fell in love with each other. 'Walk past my guards and stay with me,' said one elf. 'You know what?' said the other elf, 'What if we were to put all our guards together. They could have some fun together and protect us if necessary.' And so it happened. The two elves lived long and happily ever after. And the guards? Oh, they rarely had to save the elves, but over the years they spent more and more time on their favourite pastimes, such as making jokes, playing about, blaming each other, giving compliments and playing hide-and-seek. They had a great time. They too lived long and happily ever after.

Appendix 1
Norms and values

COMMON VALUES

- Accessibility
- Accuracy
- Alertness
- Ambition
- Assertiveness
- Autonomy
- Being market-oriented
- Being result-oriented
- Being staff-oriented
- Belief in the beauty of people
- Compassion
- Connectedness
- Cooperation
- Cost-awareness

- Courage
- Creativity
- Customer focus
- Decisiveness
- Democracy
- Dependence
- Discipline
- Drive
- Empathy
- Equality
- Excellence
- Flexibility
- Forgiveness
- Honesty

- Independence
- Initiative
- Innovation
- Integrity
- Love
- Loyalty
- Mercy
- Modesty
- Obedience
- Openness
- Quality
- Passion
- Perseverance
- Pride

- Professionalism
- Reliability
- Representativeness
- Respect
- Responsibility
- Self-esteem
- Sociability
- Social involvement
- Social responsibility
- Sustainability
- Taking responsibility
- Teamwork
- Togetherness
- Transparency

How values can be translated into norms

Ambition

Norms:

- I aim for continuous improvement
- I am constructively critical of myself
- I celebrate the results I have achieved and stop to smell the roses on the way

Togetherness

Norms:

- I am co-responsible for achieving the targets of others
- I ask for help promptly
- I make use of other people's strong points

Integrity

Norms:

- I show compassion with the receiving party
- I help the people around me to develop
- I apply my norms and values consistently

Love

Norms:

- I bring out the best in people
- I help people to help others
- I give the best I've got, without losing it

Respect

Norms:

- I see to it that others accept me the way I am
- I really listen to others so that I can understand them before I'm understood myself
- I give feedforward with a positive intention in mind

Result-orientation

Norms:

- I set clear and realistic objectives
- I do what I promise and give timely feedback
- I bring out the best in myself and the people around me

Transparency

Norms:

- I set clear expectations

- I ask questions

- I provide tailor-made information which is prompt, clear, direct, substantiated and verified

Responsibility

Norms:

- I accept the consequences of my behaviour

- I learn from the bad decisions I've made

- I think in terms of opportunities, not in terms of problems

Trust

Norms:

- I set responsibilities

- I grant powers that match the agreed responsibilities

- I provide security by allowing people to learn from their mistakes

Common restrictive norms translated into stimulating norms

You'd better (not) (behaviour)	Don't (restrictive), otherwise (fear)	Do (stimulating) because this (creation)
Ask for help	They will think you're weak	Will achieve results
Outperform others	People will become jealous	Will set an example

Hold each other to account	Will end the relationship	Strengthens the relationship
Hold the other person to account	People won't like you	Will develop the other person
Criticise	It could undermine your position	Strengthens your position when accepted
Make suggestions	You have to carry it out yourself	Will improve things
Try to make sales	You will be rejected	Will add potential value

Appendix 2
Characteristics of egos

Ego (positive)	Ego (negative)	Behaviour	Objective	Potential fears	Negative self-fulfilling prophecy in case of fear	Example of negative self-talk	Example of positive self-talk
1 Proud One	Show-off	Acquiring status by showing the other person how good you are	To be admired	Not being admired	People don't admire you because they think you're a show-off	People won't admire me if I don't show them how good I am	I will tell of my successes if this supports others
2 Independent One	Soloist	Showing others, implicitly and explicitly, that you can do it yourself, that you don't need any support or advice, that you would rather not interact with others	To retain the admiration of others	Losing your elevated position in the group (and, as a result, status)	You are not admired because people think you're too much of a soloist	I will lose people's admiration if I don't show them that I can do it by myself	By cooperating we will be able to develop further and achieve the objective sooner

Ego (positive)	Ego (negative)	Behaviour	Objective	Potential fears	Negative self-fulfilling prophecy in case of fear	Example of negative self-talk	Example of positive self-talk
3 Defender	Victim	Telling others that you're not responsible for the situation that has arisen, placing the responsibility with others, setting limits, telling others that you've got it very hard, complaining	To defend yourself, not to be held accountable or found guilty, to stand up for yourself when you are criticised, to receive compassion and sympathy	Being rejected because you are guilty or held responsible for a bad situation	You are rejected because all you do is complain, because you don't take responsibility and because people are tired of you playing the victim	I will be rejected if I take responsibility now	I'm responsible for what I do about a situation that has arisen

Ego (positive)	Ego (negative)	Behaviour	Objective	Potential fears	Negative self-fulfilling prophecy in case of fear	Example of negative self-talk	Example of positive self-talk
4 Quiet One	Dodger	Avoiding contact by not attracting attention, by not being burdened and by not risking upsetting the working relationship	To be left alone, to avoid attracting attention in order to avoid failure	Failing, and therefore being thrown out of the group	Others think that you have failed because you aren't contributing anything, so you lose your position and are thrown out of the group	Ducking my head, otherwise I might make a mistake	If my intentions are good and I bring out the best in myself, there's no reason why I shouldn't be able to join in

Ego (positive)	Ego (negative)	Behaviour	Objective	Potential fears	Negative self-fulfilling prophecy in case of fear	Example of negative self-talk	Example of positive self-talk
5 Nice One	Sweet Talker	Showing appreciation of others	To regain recognition and be part of the group	Not receiving recognition and not being allowed to be part of the group	People think that you no longer fit in because they're tired of your sweet-talking	I have to be nice, otherwise I'll be thrown out of the group	I like to express my heartfelt appreciation in order to give someone something
6 Relativist	Envious One	Downplaying the success of others	To have another person receive less recognition so that you will move up in relation to them	Receiving less recognition yourself	People do not give you as much recognition because they recognise your jealous behaviour	If I don't pull the other person from his pedestal, there won't be very much recognition left for me	I'm happy for the success of others, and their success has no bearing on mine

Ego (positive)	Ego (negative)	Behaviour	Objective	Potential fears	Negative self-fulfilling prophecy in case of fear	Example of negative self-talk	Example of positive self-talk
7 Adviser	Paternalist	Advising or trying to save others	To make yourself indispensable by helping others, thereby positioning yourself above the others	Not being indispensable	Others no longer need you because they feel that they are continually forced into an underdog position or because they are annoyed by your paternalistic behaviour	I simply must help, otherwise I'll become dispensable and be thrown out of the group	I'm happy to give advice to others when they have a need for it

Ego (positive)	Ego (negative)	Behaviour	Objective	Potential fears	Negative self-fulfilling prophecy in case of fear	Example of negative self-talk	Example of positive self-talk
8 Powerful One	Demolisher	Imposing your will by pulling others down and threatening them	To be the boss, to win, to command respect, to dominate others	That people won't respect you(r) (opinion)	People don't really respect you because they are afraid of you	I will lose authority if I don't pull the other person down	I know what I'm worth so I'll look for the best solution, instead of just advancing my solution

Appendix 3
Ego Scans©

A manager wanted to know why people in his team weren't taking any responsibility and why he had to take care of everything. He had too much going on. People were not holding each other sufficiently accountable. He hoped everything would turn out all right by organising a Giving Feed forward training course. He was also interested in the egos of all the team members. As you know, we all have powerful egos that help us to strengthen our authenticity. Everyone also has exaggerated variants of egos, which result in a negative self-fulfilling prophecy. And everyone has an allergy to other people's specific exaggerated variants. Let's look at the results of the scans.

THE MANAGER

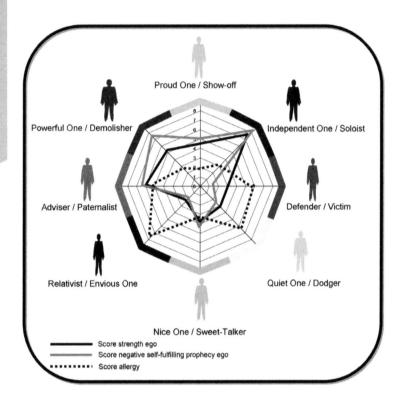

Ego Scan© of the Manager

- As you can see, this manager is very independent and powerful and likes to give other people advice.

- When he comes under greater strain and becomes concerned about his position in the group, he risks becoming a Soloist, a Demolisher and a Paternalist.

- With regard to others, he is allergic to the Envious One, the Dodger and the Victim.

THE TEAM

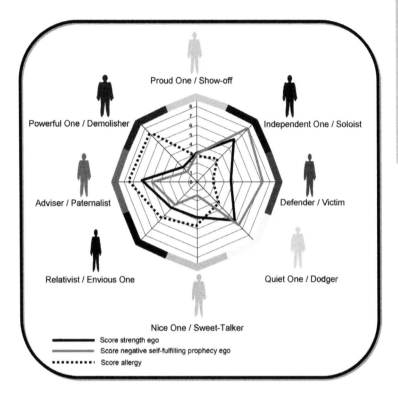

Ego Scan© of the Team

- The strong point of the team members is that they are very calm and independent and like to give other people advice.

- The exaggerated variants are the Soloist, the Victim and the Dodger.

- The allergies are the Paternalist, the Demolisher and the Envious One.

ANALYSIS

You can see that, under normal circumstances, these team members work well together. They are professionals who go about their work calmly and independently and like to give customers and each other advice. But this team came under pressure due to external circumstances. If you carefully examine the Ego Scans© and look at the manager's question, you will be able to predict what happened.

Both parties retreated into their own worlds (Soloists). The team was therefore overloaded with work, and staff members started to complain (Victims). The manager started to work even harder (Soloist) telling his team how to go about things all the time (Paternalist), while he was oblivious to their complaints (allergy to Victim). The team members had an allergic reaction to his Paternalism, since he started to build in even more checks and balances, which meant they complained even more. The manager reacted to this by bringing out the Demolisher ('Why don't they just get on with it? I'm incredibly busy as it is. I wish they'd stop moaning and just put their shoulders into it!'), as a result of which his team became even more allergic to him (one exaggerated ego triggers another). People started to complain even more ('He doesn't understand our situation and we're already working so hard'), and in turn the manager started to demolish even more, etc.

Outcome: they went their own ways (unfortunately, they were not allergic enough to the Soloist, so they simply let things take their course), creating major dissatisfaction and partially achieved results.

The solution: they looked at each other's Ego Scans©, saw where their strengths lay and recognised that the solution did not lie in the checks and balances, but in the real understanding of the situation and the expression of their need to help each other (Advisers in their prime). They then had a good laugh about each other's exaggerated egos, since it all made so much sense and was in fact quite funny. They recognised that this was not the team's deepest motive. Fear had triggered their exaggerated egos. Everyone shared the manager's mission. And they agreed to immediately give each other feedforward if they recognised an exaggerated ego (ensuring that they didn't make heavy weather of things but just identified, put an end to it and then carried on). It was a brief intervention, at the right level of abstraction. It had nothing to do with techniques, skills or competencies. Identifying egos stopped being a taboo.

The team members are cooperating well again and hold regular feedforward sessions so that they can continue to invest in each other.

Appendix 4
Twelve factors of success and failure in a cultural development programme

It appears that what are referred to as 'cultural development programmes' or 'leadership development programmes' are costly projects that rarely produce the desired results. This is why many of those who are ultimately responsible wince at the thought of launching such a programme. After an enthusiastic start, the fervour for a cultural development programme quickly fades and people carry on with business as usual. The cultural development programme fizzles out. This adds to the management's frustrations, since the culture has yet to change. The Authentic Leadership Organisational Development (ALOD) product resulted from this frustration on the part of clients (see also Appendix 5). They asked us to investigate why cultural development programmes fail, and how these programmes should be tackled using the seven layers of Authentic Leadership. This investigation yielded twelve pitfalls. We have translated them into twelve success and failure factors in a successful cultural development programme.

CULTURE

'Culture' can be defined as a set of accepted values and their corresponding norms for a particular environment. A desired (organisational) culture contributes to the organisation's mission and strategy. Most companies now realise that a 'good' culture is important for their health as far as results and staff and customer satisfaction are concerned. Cultural problems often occur after a change of strategy or market changes, or following a merger or take-over.

TWELVE FACTORS FOR SUCCESS AND FAILURE IN A CULTURAL DEVELOPMENT PROGRAMME

1. (Insufficient) staff involvement

Yet another management plaything? Calling in a lot of external parties? Don't. Involve the staff members in the definition of the desired culture. And allow your team to facilitate the process as much as possible. Staff members are likely to know what the most desired and productive culture is. Ask them to provide input, make them ambassadors, speak their language, don't use management rhetoric.

2. (Not) making cultural development measurable

Make cultural development measurable. If you don't, it won't get past the stage of good intentions (and no obligations), just lots of posters, working groups and business retreats. A culture development should support a strategy. If that's not the case, change the culture or change the strategy. Do it properly, or don't do it at all. Weak, half-hearted programmes will fall short of expectations and damage the culture. The main concern is the sustained involvement of management, since cultural issues are important but not urgent.

3. (No) model behaviour of leaders

People (subconsciously) look for reasons not to have to change since things could go wrong. Who's in the best position to give staff members the best reason not to change? That would be the leader, telling them it's all a load of nonsense. This is deadly for any cultural development process. Don't roll out until the next organisational level indicates explicitly that the managers of the level directly above it are displaying model behaviour (or making every effort to do so). Start, therefore, by empowering the managers. Analyse the egos of your managers so that they will use the powerful variant, and not leap into their exaggerated variant. And allow them to facilitate the cultural development programme using their personal mission.

4. Defining (more than) three values
You will forget the rest anyway, since we think in trigrams, unless there is a very convenient abbreviation you can use as a memory aid.

5. (No) description of restrictive and stimulating norms
The core values will be too vague for most people. Therefore, translate them into stimulating norms or rules of conduct. The norm, and not the value, defines the culture. We can quickly agree on values – everyone thinks respect is important – but are the norms for this set by giving your leader feedback or not? Also describe the restrictive norms. These are the hidden behavioural patterns that are driven by fear. Because they keep every staff member in her comfort zone, they obstruct the culture's development.

6. (Not) having an inspiring mission
A culture not only concerns norms and values. It starts with an inspiring mission. A mission is nicely put into words when, say, a colleague comes out with it spontaneously and proudly at a party. Analyse too the personal missions of individual staff members and share these; this creates a huge commitment.

7. (Not) discovering, recognising and using the management's preferred internal culture
Leaders have their own authentic culture. If their culture doesn't fit with the desired organisational culture, they will never display model behaviour, and this will negatively impact on implementation. Replace your core values or your management.

8. (Not) accepting that there are relative cultural differences between departments or locations
Different operations sometimes result in different cultures. Don't try to create a uniform whole.

9. (Not) starting with the unit that will first profit from the change

Show the rest of the organisation that the actions produce direct and measurable results and use internal facilitators. The successes will create support for a cultural development programme.

10. (No) ownership

A desired culture can only be realised if every staff member consciously commits to it and: (1) agrees with the defined norms and values; (2) wants to be held accountable for them; (3) will support them by holding others accountable for them.

11. (Not) giving each other feedforward based on the desired culture

Let every staff member participate in a feedforward session on the mission, norms and values. Don't just say you'll hold each other accountable, since that's simply not going to happen. Allow staff members to give each other specific support and facilitate this.

12. (No) coaching by managers

Allow a manager to provide coaching on concrete actions following the team's feedforward. Not providing any coaching will result in a non-committal attitude. In short, everyone needs to be involved. Allow managers to do the coaching themselves. Only call in external parties if there's no other way.

PHILOSOPHY

Culture, that's you! If you want to change a company culture, don't point to others. ALOD always focuses on individual staff members and the leaders of an organisation. Everyone should (learn to) make an optimal and measurable contribution to the realisation and maintenance of the desired culture. This means that tasks and targets will be set for each individual staff member in respect of their contribution to the cultural development process.

Appendix 5
Authentic Leadership Organisational Development (ALOD)

APPROACH

The approach consists of eight key elements:

1. Holding a fresh onlookers' *session* in which a cross-section of the organisation can give its opinion about its requirements regarding a new culture. You might choose to organise a similar session with other interest groups (customers, supervisory bodies, clients, etc.).

2. Defining a challenging *mission* and no more than *three core values* and *three stimulating norms per core value* by the highest organisational level. The outcome of the fresh onlookers' session serves, among other things, as a basis for this. In addition, an initial feedforward session based on the chosen mission, core values and norms is held with this organisational level.

3. Holding an anonymous *check* at the next organisational level. Don't roll out until the next level explicitly indicates that the managers of the level directly above it are displaying model behaviour (or making every effort to do so).

4. Holding a feedforward session with the second level, including its manager, when model behaviour is displayed. This results in *concrete actions and short-term and long-term objectives*.

5. Designing a *measuring instrument* so that the cultural development can be measured. The management can use the results to drive certain norms and values.

6. Training managers to *coach* staff members. Coaching is an important tool to bring about behavioural development and a number of staff members are trained to facilitate the further roll-out to other organisational levels.

7. Carrying out periodic *measurements*, followed up by feedforward sessions in which the results can be used for further guidance. Feedforward sessions can also be held with other stakeholders (customers, supervisory bodies, clients, etc.).

8. Implementing the mission, norms and values in the usual *HR instruments*.

Appendix 6
Authentic Leadership portrayed

We often use drawings in our consultancy work. Some of our clients have asked me to share them with readers because they portray the philosophy so well. The drawing reproduced below captures the essence of Authentic Leadership. It is a summary of the book in simple form.

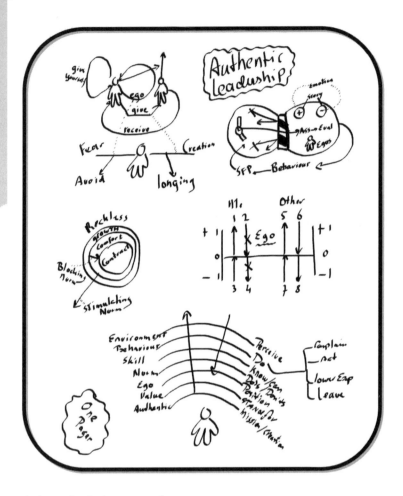

Authentic Leadership portrayed

Bibliography

Badaracco Jr., Joseph L. (2001) *Leading Quietly.* Watertown MA: Harvard Business Review Press .

Bateson, G. (1999) *Steps to an Ecology of Mind.* Chicago: University of Chicago Press.

Bazerman, Max H. & David M. Messick (1996) Ethical Leadership and the Psychology of Decision Making. *Cambridge (Massachussets):* MIT.

Boer, Bouke de (2000) *De bijzondere reis van een prikkel.* Limmen: De Prikkel.

Collins, Jim (2004) *Good to great.* New York: HarperBusiness.

Collins, Jim & J.I. Porras (2003) *Built to Last.* New York: HarperBusiness.

Covey, Stephen R. (1993) *The Seven Habits of Highly Effective People.* New York: Simon & Schuster.

Csikszentmihalyi, Mihaly (1999) *Flow.* London: Ebury Press.

Dalai Lama (2002) *Love and Compassion.* New York: Harper Collins.

Eco, Umberto, Stephen Jay Gould, Jean-Claude Carrière & Jean Delumeau (1998) *Conversations about the end of time.* New York: Fromm Intl.

Evans, Dylan (2002) *Emotion.* Oxford: Oxford University Press.

Frankl, Viktor E. (1978) *Man's search for meaning.* London: Ebury Press.

Gleick, James (2001) *The acceleration of just about everything.* New York: Pantheon Books.

Hamel, Gary & C.K. Prahalad (1994) *Competing for the future.* Watertown MA: Harvard Business Review Press.

Haring, B. (2004) *Kaas en de Evolutietheorie.* Amsterdam: Poema Pocket.

Hellinger, Bert (2001) *Love's hidden symmetry.* Phoenix: Zeig, Tucker & Theisen.

Herrmann, Ned (1996) *The whole brain business book.* New York: McGraw-Hill.

IJzermans, Theo & Coen Dirkx (1992) *Beren op de weg, spinsels in je hoofd.* Zaltbommel: Thema.

Kets de Vries, Manfred (2004) *The leadership mystique.* London: Pearson Education Limited.

Knoope, Marinus (2000) *De creatiespiraal.* Nijmegen: Uitgeverij KIC.

Koelewijn, Jannetje (2000) *Alleen winnaars overleven.* Amsterdam: Prometheus.

Kooger R. & A.N. Labohm (1999) *Conflicthantering en de onderneming.* Den Haag: Boom.

Kotter John P. (2005) *Leading Change.* Watertown MA: Harvard Business Press.

Lingsma, Marijke & Aty Boers (2004) *Scheur je los in 2005.* Soest: Uitgeverij Nelissen.

Maister, David H. (1997) *True professionalism. New York:* Free Press.

McGraw, Phillip C. (1999) *The self matters companion. New York:* Free Press.

Nadler, R. & J. Luckner (1997) *Processing the experience. Strategies to enhance and generalize learning.* Dubuque (IA): Kendall/Hunt.

Pinto, D. (1990) *Intercultural communication.* Houten/Zaventem: Bohn Stafleu Van Loghum.

Robbins, Anthony (2004) *Unlimited power.* New York: Simon & Schuster.

Rovira, Celma Álex & Trías de Bes (2004) *Good luck.* Hoboken, NJ: John Wiley & Sons Inc.

Schmid, Wilhelm (2000) *Philosophy of the art of living.* Amsterdam: Ambo.

Schulz von Thun, F. (1982) *Hoe bedoelt u?* Groningen: Wolters-Noord-hoff.

Scott Peck, M. (1978) *The road less travelled.* London: Arrow.

Seagal, Sandra & David Horne (1998) *Human Dynamics.* Waltham MA: Pegasus Communications.

Senge, Peter (2000) *The fifth discipline.* New York: Crown Business.

Skynner, Robin & John Cleese (1986) *Families and how to survive them. London:* Ebury Press.

Starren, Harry G. & Twan van de Kerkhof (2001) *De 21 geboden van modern leiderschap.* Amsterdam / Antwerpen: Business Contact.

Verhulst, Jan (1995) *Gezond verstand als therapie RET.* Lisse: Swets & Zeitlinger.

Walsch, Neale Donald (2002) *Conversations with God: An Uncommon Dialogue.* London: Hodder & Stoughton General.

Welch, Jack & Suzy Welch (2005) *Winning. New York: Harper Collins.*

Whetten, David A. & Kim S. Cameron (2002) *Developing Management Skills.* New Jersey: Prentice Hall.

Wouters, Paul (2000) *Denkgereedschap, een filosofische onderhoudsbeurt.* Rotterdam: Lemniscaat.

Index